CINDY GRAY divides her time between … she lives on the coast. There she sails … often accompanied by her daughter and … also skis, plays tennis, climbs mountai… and goes Scottish dancing wherever the… place. She isn't remotely Scottish but love… and its dancing. Her late husband, Charles, a high court judge, did not share her enthusiasm for Scottish dancing, deeming it to be 'a loathsome activity'! Cindy, by contrast, finds it hugely entertaining. An extrovert by nature, she likes the convivial nature of dancing and employed her skills as a former reporter for BBC Radio to interview fellow dancers whose comments are captured in this book. After graduating in English at Oxford University, Cindy went on to write travel articles in tandem with her career in broadcasting (under her maiden name, Selby). *Heel for Heel* is her first foray as an author.

COVER PHOTO CREDITS

Front cover:

Top left: Macgregor Gocan-Wright, mid Highland Fling, at Cowal in 2023.
Photo by Clare Marie-Bailie.

Top right: Reelers Dominica Kay-Shuttleworth and partner in 'Tulloch hold' at a St Andrew's Ball.
Photo by Isobel McTear.

Below title: Scottish Country Dancers at the Aberfeldy Highland Ball held annually at Blair Castle.
Photo by Nigel Lumsden.

Back cover:

Top: At Perth, the manly 'beaux of the ball', their arms held aloft like stags with antlers. Photo courtesy of the Perth Ball and *Scottish Field*.
Photo by Angus Blackburn.

Heel For Heel

The Story of Scottish Dance

CINDY GRAY

Luath Press Limited

EDINBURGH

www.luath.co.uk

First published 2025

ISBN: 978-1-80425-254-3

The paper used in this book is recyclable. It is made from
low-chlorine pulps produced in a low-energy,
low-emission manner from renewable forests.

FSC www.fsc.org FSC® C020637 The mark of responsible forestry

EU Ecolabel www.ecolabel.eu EU Ecolabel : SE/011/05

PEFC PEFC/05-33-99 Promoting Sustainable Forest Management www.pefc.org

Printed and bound by
Robertson Printers, Forfar

Typeset in 12 point Sabon by
Main Point Books, Edinburgh

This book is dedicated to my mother, Julianna Selby, who taught me the Highland Fling and whetted my appetite for all the genres of Scottish dancing.

Contents

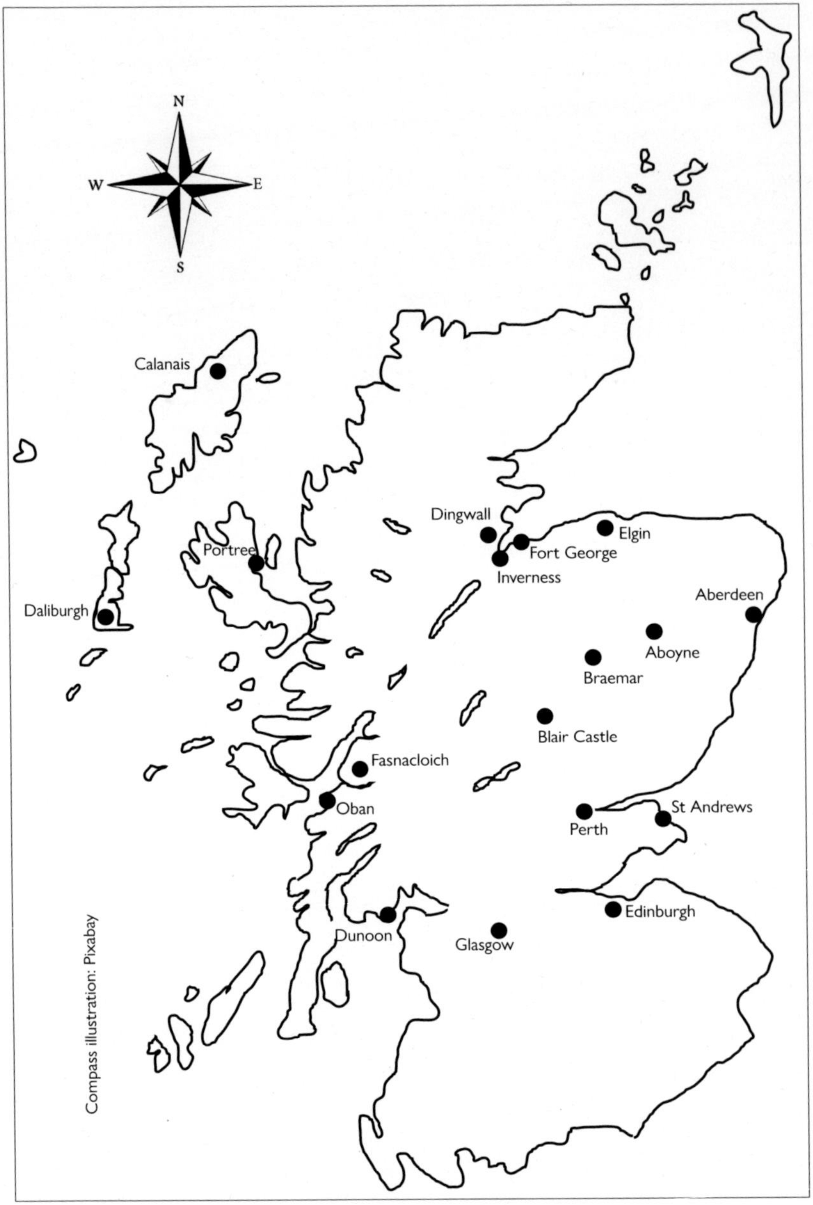

Compass illustration: Pixabay

Key Locations in the Story of Dance in Scotland

ABERDEEN: good location for ceilidhs and with an active RSCDS programme (Royal Scottish Country Dance Society)

ABOYNE: one of the Highland Ball venues along with Inverness (for Northern Meeting), Stirling, Skye, Donside, Angus, Oban, Lochaber and Perth

BLAIR CASTLE: at Blair Atholl and the venue for Aberfeldy and other Highland balls

BRAEMAR: Highland Dancing is an integral part of the Braemar Gathering held annually in September

CALANAIS: 5,000-year-old circle of standing stones overlooking Loch Roag on the Isle of Lewis, whose arrangement is possibly suggestive of ancient Celtic dance traditions

DALIBURGH: township in South Uist and home to Ceòlas, an annual summer school celebrating all things Gaelic, including Step Dance

DINGWALL: formerly the location for Mrs Grant's dance school teaching traditional reels

DUNOON: small town on western shore of upper Firth of Clyde and home, in late August, to the Cowal Gathering incorporating the World Highland Dancing Championship

EDINBURGH: the base for the RSCDS and also Stockbridge Reelers

ELGIN: formerly the location for Miss Matthews' dance school teaching traditional reels

FASNACLOICH: home to Ysobel Stewart, co-founder of the RSCDS, on marriage to Ian Charles Stewart of Fasnacloich in 1909

FORT GEORGE: large 18th century fortress near Ardersier and occasional venue for Northern Meeting balls

GLASGOW: home of Jean Milligan, co-founder of the RSCDS, and venue for Kelvingrove Step Dance classes

INVERNESS: former venue for Northern Meeting balls, now held in various locations in the countryside around Inverness

OBAN: venue for Argyllshire Gathering ball and also Highland Dancing

PERTH: base for reeling balls since 1820 with balls now being held further afield e.g. Blair Castle, Scone Palace, Fingask Castle

PORTREE: on Isle of Skye and the base for the Skye Ball, established in 1877, held on two consecutive nights in September

ST ANDREWS: base for the RSCDS Summer School and thriving university SCD and reeling societies

Young reelers in Tulloch hold at a St Andrew's Ball in 2023
Photo: Isobel McTear

Introduction

ON ANY SATURDAY in late August there's a flurry of tartan. Highland Dancers gathered at Dunoon in Scotland polish their shoes and check their kilts for the final heats of the Cowal Gathering. Reelers heading to the Northern Meeting dust off tartan sashes and kilts or trews. Scottish Country Dancers from Fife to Sydney assemble their sporrans and finery and convene at summer parties. Brides and grooms celebrating with a ceilidh supervise the hanging of tartan banners and the bows in the bridesmaids' hair. These festivities happen all over the world and at other key moments in the year: St Andrew's Day in November, Burns Night in January, spring breaks…

It's not just tartan – and whisky – that Scotland exports. It's the dancing. I myself, aged seven, performed the Highland Fling with another child in Djakarta, Indonesia, to showcase British culture. Recently I've met teenagers in the Falkland Islands dancing 'Strip the Willow' and youths from America, Canada and Australia assembling worldwide for Highland Dance competitions. Apart from Antarctica, every continent has groups of Scottish dancers. There are the reelers who spin

Young piper in the town hall at Daliburgh, South Uist, in July 2024
Ceòlas

round the floor doing ten well-known dances like 'Hamilton House'. Scottish Country Dancers, meanwhile, cover a wider range of reels as well as jigs and slower Strathspeys. Ceilidh dancers congregate at urban gyms and church or village halls where a caller introduces the simple moves of the ceilidh dances. Highland dancers are the younger ones leaping around on a stage, whilst other enthusiasts of fancy footwork opt for the recently revived Scottish Step Dance gaining momentum in pubs and at festivals.

Whichever the genre of Scottish dancing, it is, of course, a very tactile activity. It therefore slumped during Covid. But since we resumed getting up close and personal, this type of dancing is more popular than ever. Throughout the world millions of people do it – from children aged three to nonagenarians. What is its appeal?

Certainly, one of the main attractions of Scottish dancing is the music that goes with it. The steady beat and catchy tunes – played on fiddles, accordions, bagpipes – make one long to stand up and dance. Of course, other national dances have pulsating music. Spanish flamenco, Russian Cossack, Argentinian tango, Egyptian belly-dancing come to mind. But whilst those (and competitive Highland dancing) tend to be solo performances showing off highly complicated steps and gymnastic feats, most Scottish dancing is easy to learn and a sociable activity. Everyone dances with everyone else; grandparents swirl their grandchildren, men flirt with women, people of all orientations feel at ease, potential wallflowers and bystanders are swept onto the floor. The dances are progressive, so each pair has a turn at the top of a set, each man or woman has a go in the middle of a circle, nobody is more important than anyone else. Scottish dancing is truly all-embracing and democratic.

It also keeps you fit. In 2010, a team from the University of Strathclyde, Glasgow, carried out a fascinating study of 70 elderly women, all of whom were physically active. They were divided into two groups: Scottish dancers and non-dancers. That research – and other studies with participants of all ages and both sexes – show that the dancers walk faster, are more flexible and have greater muscle strength than active people who don't dance. Moreover, dancing of all kinds is known to reduce anxiety, depression and the risk of dementia. Thinking on your feet could be better than medicine!

This book is not a manual – though I have listed instruction booklets and websites as well as places where you can learn and participate. It is a joyful celebration of Scottish dancing across all the genres: from the Highland Fling which started in the Scottish Highlands centuries ago to the evolving reels, Scottish Country Dancing, ceilidhs and Step Dance which later spread across the whole of Scotland, and thence worldwide. I focus on all the people involved in Scottish dancing: the bagpipers, bandleaders, kilt-makers and everyone, young or old, who likes a fling – of the Scottish variety!

Right: Reelers spinning at a ball at the Hurlingham Club in London
Photo: Isobel McTear

Step we gaily, on we go,
Heel for heel and toe for toe,
Arm in arm and row on row,
All for Mairi's wedding.

Like the 'Mairi's Wedding' song – and the dance that goes with it – *Heel for Heel* captures the fun of Scottish dancing. The book is not an instruction manual or a comprehensive history. Rather, it homes in on the people who enjoy all the genres of Scottish dancing, as outlined below.

Scottish Country Dancing (SCD): this covers the numerous traditional and more modern Scottish dances as spread worldwide by the Royal Scottish Country Dance Society (RSCDS). The dances include slow Strathspeys and faster jigs and reels, all performed neatly.

Reeling: the term given to the more energetic kind of social dancing, focusing on the ten most popular Scottish dances and incorporating vigorous spinning.

Ceilidh: a gathering with the simplest of all the dances – ideal for teenagers at parties, villagers at harvest suppers and guests at weddings.

Highland Dancing: the earliest form of Scottish dancing, including 'The Sword Dance' and 'Highland Fling'. Originally danced by warriors, now by young people at festivals and competitions. Requires intricate footwork, agility and grace.

Step Dance: a hard-shoe, percussive dance similar to Irish Sean-Nós (as in *Riverdance*) but with a more relaxed upper body. Step Dance went from Scotland to Nova Scotia and is now resurfacing in its birthplace.

CHAPTER ONE

A Brief History

NOBODY KNOWS HOW Scottish dancing started. On the Isle of Lewis in the Outer Hebrides are the Calanais Standing Stones erected 5,000 years ago. Some historians believe that Druids, the learned class amongst the ancient Celts, organised rituals associated with astronomy, worship and dance. Certainly, the arrangement of stones – in a circle around one prominent central pillar – foreshadows the Eightsome Reel which emerged centuries later as well as dancing round a Maypole which dates back to the 12th century and was a pagan celebration of fertility. The pole symbolises a phallus.

Calanais standing stones with one central prominent pillar
VisitScotland. Photo: Kenny Lam

Medieval dancers accompanied by musicians, including a piper
The British Library, Cotton MS Cleopatra C VIIIf 19v

The return of spring, midsummer and harvest were all good reasons to make merry in medieval times and there is evidence (for instance, in Anglo-Saxon manuscripts) that dancing was popular. In those hard times (from 1066 to 1485 in Britain) there wasn't much else to do that was fun, like dancing, or so effective at warming you up – quite a consideration on the chilly moors and in the draughty castles of Scotland.

Many of the early dances would have been known in other parts of Europe. They were part of the folk tradition spread by travelling minstrels, gypsies and tinkers. In a different league was the battlefield Sword Dance, mentioned in documents going back to the 11th-century reign of King Malcolm III of Scotland. He allegedly was so pleased on defeating a rival chieftain at a battle in 1054, that he lay his opponent's sword on the ground, crossed it with his own and skipped around them. After this the Sword Dance was traditionally performed by Scottish warriors on the eve of battle, taking

The Sword Dance – or, in Gaelic, the 'Ghillie Callum'
Dumfries Museum

care to avoid touching the blades (deemed unlucky) whilst another ancient dance, the Highland Fling, signified victory following a battle. Fighters danced on top of their upturned shields, each with a sharp spike of steel projecting from the centre. You couldn't put a foot wrong! Both the Sword Dance and the Highland Fling tested and built up the strength, agility and accuracy of warriors (and their modern successors, the Highland dancers).

Separately more sociable dances were gaining ground at court. Longwise sets, with pairs of dancers facing each other in two rows, were arranged by the Stewart kings. In December 1580 it was noted in the *Accounts of the Lord High Treasurer of Scotland* that King James VI paid £100 to a man called William Hudson for 'teaching us to dance'. Mary Queen of Scots, having lived in France, introduced a few French dances and, from the Basque region, the enduring '*Pas de Basque*' step (hopping from right to left). Meanwhile the 'ring' dance continued to be a great favourite with country folk, often danced in fields at harvest time accompanied by bagpipes. Despite the Scottish church's disapproval of anything jolly – in particular, dancing (associated with witchcraft) – it was described by dancing-master Kellom Tomlinson in his *Art of Dancing*, 1735, as 'the Darling or favourite diversion of all Ranks of People from the Court to the Cottage'.

While the holier-than-thou Calvinists failed to eradicate this 'favourite diversion', a greater threat came with the Act of Proscription following the Battle of Culloden in 1746. For 36 years until the Act was repealed in 1782, the English government sought to purge the Highlands of its clans for fear of rebellion. Tartan, bagpipes, Scottish dancing were all outlawed. The mere act of wearing a kilt or carrying a dagger or any other weapon was a penal offence. The Act had a severe impact on Highland dancing, which needed the garb and props that had been banned. But other genres of Scottish dancing continued behind the closed doors of castles, in remote rural spots and increasingly in assembly rooms, constructed to accommodate the sets of country dance.

By the 1780s Edinburgh, Aberdeen, Glasgow, Inverness, Dundee and Leith had all acquired spacious assemblies.

Edinburgh Assembly – a popular venue for Scottish dancing in the 18th century

Alamy

'Dancies' (itinerant dancing-masters) and booklets containing directions for the dances and music to accompany them helped spread the word, the first Scottish collection being written by John Bowie and published in Perth in 1789. Manuscripts of individual dances, for example 'The Duke of Perth' (dated 1737), also illustrate how popular Scottish dancing had become in 18th-century Scotland. The prosperous flocked to the elegant, spacious assemblies. Others made do, with equal enthusiasm, with village halls and country barns. Robert Burns, the son of a tenant farmer, attended a dancing school in his youth and remarked in a letter to George Thomson in 1794 that he derived 'exquisite enjoyment' from 'Strathspeys ancient and modern'.

Peculiarly, the English who had sought to suppress everything Jacobite and clannish in the mid 18th century were the very people who sparked a revival in Scottish culture in the 19th century. In 1805, dancing master Thomas Peacock of Aberdeen described 'the rage which for some time past has prevailed in England for the national dances of the Scotch, especially their Reel'. King George IV visited Edinburgh in 1822 wearing a kilt and was well received (despite looking ridiculous as his kilt was much too short). His niece, Queen Victoria, wore tartan with more flair, loved Scotland and Scottish traditions and attended Highland Games with Highland dancing back on the programme. She employed a dancing master, Joseph Lowe, who in 1852 recorded in his diary teaching the whole royal family 'the Reel of Eight... Her Majesty thought it great fun and entered quite into the spirit of it'.

King George IV 'Equipt for a Northern visit', 1822 cartoon
Edinburgh City Council

After the Napoleonic Wars ended in 1815 there was a craze in Europe for two new dances: the waltz and the quadrille. Those, however, did not eclipse Scottish dancing but were simply incorporated into it. Whilst country dancing declined elsewhere in Europe, it continued to flourish in Scotland partly because military regiments engaged in it and the gentry

Queen Victoria, who loved everything Scottish, in tartan sash
Alamy

supported it. In England, too, the grandees enjoyed exuberant Hunt Balls and in 1851 the first Royal Caledonian Ball was held in London attracting reelers from both sides of the border.

'The Emigrants'

The Emigrants, 1844, London, by William Allsworth. The painting, now in the collection of the Museum of New Zealand, Te Papa Tongawera in Wellington, depicts a family in the Scottish Highlands gathered with all their livestock and luggage, ready to depart on a ship offshore which bears the 1835 flag of New Zealand.

Te Papa (1992-0022-1)

Simultaneously, all types of Scottish dancing spread to the New World. The Highland and Lowland Clearances (1750–1860) and the Potato Famine of 1846 prompted thousands of Scots to emigrate to Canada, the Americas, Australia and New Zealand.They took with them their culture, including dancing. In Canada, for instance, which to this day has the highest level of Scottish descendants per capita in the world, there are flourishing groups of Scottish Country Dancers, reelers and Highland dancers, while Step Dance prevails in Nova Scotia, the Latin term for 'New Scotland'.

Back in the motherland there was a period in the 20th century when Scottish dancing could have foundered. After the First World War, jazz was the hot favourite. The hunt ball at Perth retained a few reels, the Glasgow Police ball some Scottish Country Dances. But traditional dances were in decline. Even at the celebrated Northern Meeting in Inverness the music for the ball was provided, in 1923, by the Yahoo Jazz Sextet!

Mercifully, in that very same year two women, Ysobel Stewart and Jean Milligan, called a public meeting which led to the foundation of the Scottish Country Dance Society. That was a crucial turning point destined to make Scotland dance again to its own music. Over a hundred years later, Scottish dancing has spread worldwide due to the unstinting efforts of Jean Milligan in particular. Although most of the chapters in this book focus on living, lively dancers, Miss Milligan is one character from the past whose vitality and consequent achievements warrant more than a passing mention.

It was an enterprising music publisher, Michael Diack, who introduced the genteel Mrs Ysobel Stewart of Fasnacloich to Miss Jean Milligan of Glasgow, a professional sports and dance teacher. For some time after the First World War,

Portrait of Jean Milligan, co-founder of the Scottish Country Dance Society.
Painted c1961 by Henry Raeburn Dobson
RSCDS archives

Jean Milligan had recognised the value of sociable Scottish dancing for the thousands of women aptly described as the 'war widows who had never been married'. 'Here's something that's fun,' she said, 'and that doesn't need men.' Her early classes were attended mainly by women, though she later brought in men by making Scottish dancing part of the course for all Physical Education teachers. But when Jean Milligan met Ysobel Stewart, their joint concern was for the future of Scottish dancing which looked as though it might be completely ousted by foxtrots and jazz, and which anyway had become chaotic and rough. They placed a notice in the *Glasgow Herald* inviting anyone interested in 'Scots Country Dances' to attend a meeting in the Athenaeum (now the Hard Rock Café) on Monday 26th November 1923 at 5.00pm. Jean Milligan later recalled how she and Ysobel Stewart, before the appointed hour, whispered dubiously to each other, 'Do you think anyone will come?' In fact, 27 people turned up; a busy meeting ensued as did the Scottish Country Dance Society. Its aim was to preserve the old dances and dance music of Scotland, to publish booklets describing the dances and to encourage people to learn them.

In pursuit of those goals Jean was indefatigable. Before publishing each booklet, she would hunt down the earliest known steps and formations of the various dances and spend hours at the piano trying out tunes to accompany them. Both she and Mrs Stewart set up classes, including ones for potential teachers, conducted examinations of candidates and, in 1927, inaugurated a Summer School at St Andrews which is still going strong a hundred years later.

Music publisher Michael Diack, who played a key role in setting up the RSCDS
Royal Scottish Country Dance Society (RSCDS) archives

Mrs Ysobel Stewart of Fasnacloich, co-founder of the Scottish Country Dance Society

RSCDS archives

Long after Ysobel Stewart retired, Jean Milligan carried on with the mission. She travelled extensively, teaching and demonstrating Scottish dances. As a result, if you go to Japan, Canada, Australia or South Africa, you'll find groups dancing, say, 'Mairi's Wedding' in exactly the same way as anyone in Scotland. Before Jean Milligan, Scottish dancing had descended into 'rowdy romps'. She urged people to 'dance with your soul' but with 'controlled abandon'. And she got what she wanted.

Jean was an extraordinary character. She was not at all self-conscious. In her First Aid post during the Glasgow blitz of 1943, when there was a shortage of steel helmets, Jean carried on cheerfully wearing a tea cosy on her head with an enamel basin on top!

She showed her mettle again in 1946 when she took 66 dancers to Wembley for a festival. The arena was so vast the dancers were far removed from the Scots Guards band and they were out of kilter at the start. Undaunted by an audience of 40,000 people, Miss Milligan marched into the arena, shouted, 'Stop! Stop!' and then, by using her voice and arms, managed to get the band and dancers to begin again, this time in perfect unison!

She continued teaching, adjudicating and promoting Scottish dancing well into her 80s, though she never divulged her exact age. To a New Zealand reporter she said, 'I am getting old and I am getting lame, but in my heart I am full of dancing.' Jean's long life is chronicled in the biography *Dance with Your Soul* by Alastair MacFadyen and Florence Adams (RSCDS 1983).

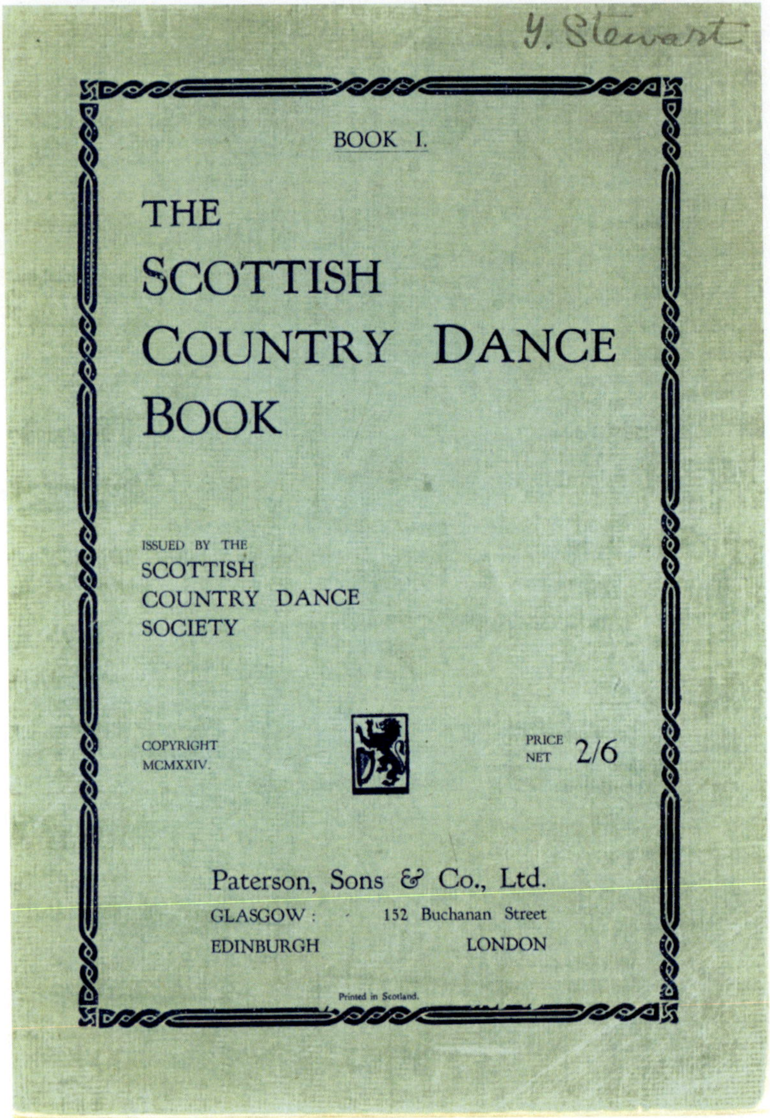

The first Scottish Country Dance booklet, published in January 1924. This particular copy belonged to Ysobel Stewart (signature top right)

RSCDS archives

'The Triumph', 1945, Jean Milligan and friends at 'Summer School' in St Andrews
RSCDS archives

Summer School in 1947 when the hot, dry weather led to dancing outdoors
RSCDS archives

'Jean at the Ready', with headgear, during the Blitz
Cartoon by Roddy Martine

Jean Milligan in Toronto in the 1950s
RSCDS archives

We owe a lot to Jean Milligan and to her fellow associate, Ysobel Stewart, for consolidating and refining how we dance today. The society they founded, which, under

Jean Milligan in New Zealand
RSCDS archives

Dancers in South Africa, 1960
RSCDS archives

the patronage of King George VI in 1951, became the Royal Scottish Country Dance Society, marked its centenary in 2023 by making a video of people in Britain and abroad dancing 'The Flying Scotsman' since the train of that name was also 100 years old. Critics of the RSCDS, who consider that Jean Milligan may have made Scottish Country Dancers too 'pointy-toed' and precise with fussy renditions of obscure

'Flying Scotsman' as danced in 2023 in Richmond, Yorkshire
Richmond, North Yorkshire branch of RSCDS

dances, should look at the 'Flying Scotsman' video. It is a wonderful celebration of a simple dance performed with controlled abandon on streets, beaches and stages in every corner of the globe.

CHAPTER TWO

Scottish Country Dancing and People Who Do It

SCOTTISH COUNTRY DANCING (SCD) – as championed by Jean Milligan – evolved from English Country Dance formations combined with Highland steps and music. The word 'country' may have derived from the supposed rustic origins or from the French word '*contre*' meaning 'opposite', since SCD often involves longwise 'sets' or rows of couples facing each other. There are usually three or more couples in each set, with all the men (or 'leaders') lined up on one side facing the ladies (or 'followers') on the other. Apart from longwise sets, some dances are shaped like triangles (with three couples, one in each corner) or squares (with four couples on the sides of a square). The accompanying music is either fast, as in jigs or reels, or more slow and stately for Strathspeys. At balls and parties, a waltz or march may be added to the mix.

A dance teacher at a school or hall, a caller at a ceilidh and an MC at a ball will often ask people to 'make up sets'. This simply means 'please go onto the floor and get into specified groups.' But there is also the verb 'to set', which is the noted *Pas de Basque* step whereby one dancer faces another and skips to right and left on the spot. There's a travel step, too, in order to progress from one place to another and a slip step used to travel sideways – for instance, when you're dancing in a circle. More complicated steps include the Highland

Schottische, whilst there are dozens of moves like 'casting off', 'setting to corners', 'rights and lefts', promenades and allemandes (originally from the continent) and 'four hands across' – more commonly known as 'teapots'.

Formation known as 'teapots' as depicted in *The Swinging Sporran*

Even more daunting for novices is the sheer number of dances, over 11,000! They range from very easy ones like 'Dunnet Head' to complicated 'Nottingham Lace' and 'Bonnie Anne' (which is as bonny as its name). There are several with peculiar titles – for instance, two by the prolific dance deviser John Drewry (1923–2014) called 'There Be Dragons' and 'The Bees of Maggieknockater'. The latter was famously performed in Banff, Alberta, in 1983 by dancers

John Drewry, dance deviser and hillwalker – John enjoyed scrambling up the hills of Cumbria and Scotland, snow was no deterrent
RSCDS archives

dressed in yellow and black striped costumes while an ageing Queen Bee wielded a tennis racket to keep the drones buzzing, all to the tune of Rimsky Korsakov's 'Flight of the Bumblebee'! However, whilst the vast repertoire of dances means that experts can be forever challenged, total beginners can still enjoy SCD once they've dipped a toe in the water.

Toes are to the point in SCD – that is, regular participants usually point them, curving the front of the foot towards the floor. To that end, both men and women wear soft-soled shoes for formal dances and the same supple footwear or, at least, flat trainers for practices. Reelers, who dance ten of the 11,000 Scottish Country Dances, and guests at ceilidhs with a handful of SCD on the programme wear all sorts of shoes. But if, like me, you've had a woman's stiletto or the hard heel of a hefty man land on your foot, then one sees the merit of everyone wearing traditional 'ghillies' or 'pumps' (the soft-soled shoes) which, if they've also got some shock absorbing insoles, enable one to dance for hours without getting tired.

For all kinds of Scottish dancing there are likely to be some men wearing kilts and others in tartan 'trews', a variety of

jackets and sporrans and a small dagger, a Sgian Dubh (left, pronounced 'Skeendoo'), tucked in a sock. Women get off more lightly with skirts and dresses, long at balls, sometimes with a tartan sash pinned over the left shoulder (or right shoulder if the woman is a 'somebody', eg an army officer's wife). At informal events and practices any loose, comfortable clothes are the norm.

From its former links with French dancing, SCD looks neater and more balletic than reeling and ceilidh dancing. There is also less yeoching (loud whooping) and birling (swift spinning) than at reels or ceilidhs. French etiquette prevails, like bowing or curtseying to your partner and joining others already on the floor at the end of the lines, never in the middle just because your friends are standing there. Yet despite a degree of formality in SCD, its governing organisation, the RSCDS, based in Edinburgh, is keen to promote the activity for its three undoubted, unconstrained benefits: fun, fitness and friendship. Those attributes were at the forefront of the society's centenary celebrations in 2023

Tartan trews or kilts with sporrans are traditional wear for male Scottish dancers when William Williamson was president.

William epitomises the more relaxed attitude of today's Scottish Country Dancer. Having started at the age of five with a RSCDS teacher in Dumfries, he went on to rural gatherings, joined a ceilidh band and has played both for ceilidhs and reeling parties. At those, he says, 'There's less emphasis on neat footwork but I go to them all and enjoy myself. I've always disliked pigeonholing SCD, reels, ceilidhs. None of us should get uppity and consider ourselves superior to other kinds of dancers. That's just nonsense. 'The Reel of the 51st Division', the 'Duke of Perth'... we all dance them, just in different styles. But so what? Each type has its merits but it all has the same roots.'

William believes in the old adage, 'When in Rome do as the Romans do.' He adjusts his style of dancing in keeping with others around him. Some members of the RSCDS hierarchy have not necessarily been as open-minded as him. In 1996 when Peter Knight, an SCD tutor based in England, asked the society to publish his reference booklet *Scottish Country Dancing*, he was met with reluctance and antipathy towards newcomers and reelers. Peter recalls the RSCDS response: 'Why should we publish a book to teach them how to do our dances wrong?' The booklet was eventually published in association with the RSCDS, but William Williamson has no idea why the society was initially so negative. 'That attitude has gone,' he explains, 'We're a much more open organisation now, reaching out to other cultural organisations, dance and musical groups.' When I met him, he was setting off to meet the National Association of Accordion and Fiddle Clubs, with dates in his diary to award a trophy at the Festival for Celtic Connection for the best Scottish dance band.

The main challenge during his tenure was Covid. He and his team at the RSCDS were worried that SCD would fizzle out. But by using Zoom and 'teaching from our living rooms people joined in from all over the world.' Before the pandemic there were 9,000 members worldwide. There's the same number once again (plus thousands more in affiliated groups) and unabated enthusiasm. 'Of course, we've got competition,' he continues, 'There is so much entertainment on tap. There are gyms everywhere and people can dip in and out of them or just stay at home playing with gadgets.' Where SCD has the edge is with social interaction. Anyone can stroll into a hall where a class is taking place, whether or not they have a partner, then dance with everyone, make new friends and keep fit in the process.

I wondered if the membership was ageing. 'Definitely not,' William replied, 'We have an older age group which is no bad thing since SCD keeps people mentally and physically fit into their 80s and 90s. But I've just come back from the Newcastle Festival where there were about 130 young people (late teens and twenty-year-olds) doing SCD very enthusiastically.'

Amongst the 300 RSCDS branches abroad are several which attract younger cohorts including an active group in Lyon, France. William takes pride in the range of ages and countries which the RSCDS embraces. 'We've all got international, life-long friends. You go to a ball abroad and bump into people you've met in other countries ages ago.'

A Burns Night ball with tartan banners at the Hurlingham Club, London

He adds, touchingly, 'Many dancers will tell you that their SCD friends are the ones they can rely on, who have got them through hard times. However, we're not a clique. It's not a question of, "Watch us. This is what we do." It's, "Come and join us!"... even if it's just for a blether.'

For decades (until I took over in 2010) Gilly Nester-Smith ran the dancing at London's prestigious Hurlingham Club with her friend, Peter Knight, as tutor at the classes and MC at the balls. Gilly learnt the main reels at her school, Tudor Hall, and later added SCD to her repertoire. She likes both genres and would, for instance, often have 'The Hurlingham Quadrangle' (devised by Peter) on the programme, but she also organised reels including a memorable 'Thirtytwosome'

Gilly-Nester-Smith (left), former organiser of Scottish dancing at the Hurlingham Club, London

('The Eightsome' quadrupled) at a Concours d'Elegance on the club's immaculate lawn in 1991.

There was the occasional blip. Gilly recalls a Burns Night when she had to reprimand a youth who had smuggled in an illicit bottle of whisky. She was dismayed not so much by the deed as his lack of manners. 'When I was talking to him, he didn't stand up!' she told me in consternation.

Although Gilly has high standards, she is not in the least high and mighty. When I asked if she had Scottish roots her husband, Laci, prompted her to mention that her uncle had left her a castle in Scotland. 'Only a little one,' added Gilly hastily, 'and atrocious with no electricity.' Not surprisingly, she had to let that go and her dancing shoes are also gathering dust. Yet her legacy continues at the leafy club in south-west London with Scottish dancing still on the programme. I asked her why the activity itself appealed to her. 'It's inclusive,' she replied, 'and for all ages. In today's fragmented society, Scottish dancing is the glue.'

The inclusive nature of Scottish dancing is certainly on display at the Gay Gordons sessions which are affiliated to the RSCDS and operate, in the UK, in London, Edinburgh and Manchester.s

At St Andrews I met Murrough Landon, one of the teachers at the London branch. Like its counterparts in the UK and elsewhere, the London Gay Gordons is for the LGBTQI+ community. The acronym stands, respectively, for Lesbian, Gay, Bisexual, Transgender, Queer/Questioning and Intersex. Some organisations add an 'A' for Asexual. At its Wednesday evening sessions, the London branch attracts up

A Gay Gordons session

to 16 dancers with many more men than women. Murrough mentioned that heterosexual people sometimes join them. 'The other evening we had a married couple. The husband danced on the women's side, the wife on the men's just to ring the changes!'

The London GGs was kickstarted in October 2005 by Daniel Capron, who Murrough Landon introduced to John Tyler at Dancerama (a week of dancing for lesbians and gay men held at Laurieston Hall in Scotland). John Tyler readily came on board with Daniel to launch the first GG dance group and was the ideal co-founder, being a qualified Scottish Country Dance teacher; as a young man he was examined by and got his certificate from an elderly Jean Milligan! John was an inspirational teacher and both the classes in London and subsequent full weeks of Gay Gordons SCD at Laurieston Hall were successful. In 2015 Murrough Landon conveyed the group's appreciation for the founders by devising a Strathspey for them: 'Gorgeous Gordons' – 'for John and Daniel ten years on'. A decade later, the members continue to dance and socialise.

Manchester Gay Gordons started in 2008 with Dave Taylor at the helm. That group dances in the upstairs bar of a pub and they have had fundraising dances for Water Aid, the Children's Hospital and other charities. The Edinburgh group, launched by Turan Ali and tutor Tim Bolton-Maggs, had its first gathering in 2009 on the upper floor of a Quaker Friends Meeting House. Turan recalls that 'the floor shook and wobbled from so many of us dancing!' Despite having to change venue time and again, the Edinburgh 'Kilt Nights' with live music remain popular. All the UK Gay Gordons feel a sense of achievement in that they have managed to arrange dances where being queer is the norm. Moreover, at regular events, including RSCDS ones, where for years 'spare' women have paired up, it is no longer frowned upon if two men partner each other.

Just one vexed question remains: what to call everybody. Traditionally, looking towards the band, men stand on the left, women on the right and men lead the way. Adopting gender-neutral language, the Gay Gordons initially called those standing on the left 'leaders', those on the right, 'followers'. Several variations arose. The Edinburgh Gay Gordons had the 'men', called Tartans, wearing tartan bands and the 'women', called Rainbows, wearing rainbow-coloured bands. London also adopted bands (sashes worn across the chest) but then abandoned them after Covid.

In America there was a strong move for a rhythmic structure, the appellations having the same number of syllables as 'men' and 'women' – hence 'larks' for the men on the left and 'ravens' for women on the right. But nobody fancied being a raven, so that was replaced with robin. A well-known dance musician had spent a long time transitioning from a man to a woman and had finally achieved her goal, being very sceptical about all the 'larks' and 'robins'. This individual ruefully declared, 'I've gone through untold trauma in order to become a woman. I don't want to be a bloody robin!'

A further complication is that all the crib sheets for dances have the abbreviations M for men, W for women. Changing all of those to L for Larks, R for Robins would be no mean feat. So, somebody came up with yet another idea: Moles (= men) and Wombats (= women). Needless to say, that never took off!

CHAPTER THREE

Teaching the Dance

I'VE HAD A blether (or chat) with hundreds of Scottish Country Dancers both in the UK and, latterly, abroad. I was curious to know how foreign societies organise and teach their SCD and what their compatriots think of it.

In Lyon, France, Raphaelle Orgeret runs three classes a week: two on Mondays for 'kids and teenagers', another on Friday for mixed abilities and all ages. She organises a music and dance workshop in November, a Christmas ceilidh, a Burns Night dance and a big weekend in April, sometimes in a *château*, with a class for under-30-year-olds and another for those aged over 30. She herself is spurred on by the enthusiasm of the youngsters, four of whom she is training to become SCD teachers to ensure the future of the group. France has long been keen on Scotland so its national dancing meets with general approval. 'Friends of ours who haven't danced,' says Raphaelle, 'are pretty enthusiastic. Some think it's cool, some come and try.'

Across the pond, of course, SCD is less of a novelty. Because so many Scots emigrated to Canada and the USA, Scottish culture (including dancing) has been widespread for centuries. Currently there are about 37 branches in Canada and 50 in the USA. Those are the official RSCDS branches, each of which could have several groups attached to them.

Then there are two dozen affiliated groups and others outside of the RSCDS. Fiona Miller, based in Lethbridge, Canada, and chair of TAC, the worldwide SCD Teachers Association, describes 'children's classes starting at age four, seniors' classes going up to 98-year-olds and everything in between.' There are dances for St Andrew's Day and Burns Night, and teacher training summer schools. For Fiona, the particular appeal of SCD is its 'patterns, symmetry and the music itself but most of all the socialising. I also get to travel the world because of the dancing. My non-dancing friends think it's great and enjoy coming to watch at special events or participating when we have public events.'

A special event in San Francisco, USA, is the Valentine's Ball in February. The dozen San Francisco RSCDS groups amalgamate, mustering around 275 guests for the dance, the women wearing long dresses, the men sporting kilts. I met one regular participant, Sheila Shain, from the Walnut Creek suburb of San Francisco. She happily signs up for the February gathering as well as the weekly Scottish Country Dance classes in Berkeley, Crockett or Danville and the party on the first Saturday of every winter month. Sheila also plans to attend the SCD weekend at Asilomar Beach in Monterey, relishing the friendly atmosphere and the inherent fun of dancing.

Before a tango show in Buenos Aires I had the pleasure of meeting Charly Candia and Maria Sol Grimaldi who together head up a SCD group in Argentina's capital. They started 20 years ago, having been inspired by a prized long-haul trip to Scotland for the Summer School at St Andrews.

Members of the Buenos Aires Scottish Country Dance Group at the 2024 Summer School in St Andrews

Their sessions in Buenos Aires start in March, when it's cooler, and they carry on until December with a class every Friday for beginners to intermediates and another on Sunday for experienced dancers who, in turn, often attend the Friday lessons to help the novices. Using the RSCDS booklets they cover a wide range of dances including, recently, 'Diamond Jubilee', 'Pelorus Jack', 'Scallywag' and 'City Lights'. In October, they head 17 miles north of Buenos Aires to Delta Tigre where, like another dance in their repertoire, it's 'Light and Airy', being on the banks of a river. Here they dance all morning in a hall then have a waterside barbecue and go

St Andrews from the beach
Photo: Cassandra Miller

rowing. Charly, the organiser, and Maria Sol, the tutor, admit that their fellow Argentinians think SCD is 'a bit weird'. But they and their 30 followers love it – in particular, the 'Happy Meeting' at Delta Tigre.

Charly Candia and two other Argentinians were amongst the many foreign and British dancers at the 2024 RSCDS Summer School, which I also attended. This was the society's 91st summer school held annually since 1927 apart from during the Second World War and the two years of Covid. The enduring popularity of the summer school prompted the RSCDS to launch a Winter one as well in 2000. This is now an annual fixture, taking place in Pitlochry. The venue for the summer school is St Andrews, a Scottish seaside university town whose student rooms in the long vacation are available to accommodate dancers. They, in turn, usually opt for one week of the four-week residential, fully catered courses (from mid-July to mid-August). St Andrews is also blessed with a famous golf course, three fine beaches, ancient buildings and, most importantly, several large halls with wooden floors – ideal for dancing.

The evening social dances take place in the enormous, grand Younger Hall or in the Common Room of University Hall – the latter also being the space for classes along with the Town Hall and Victory Memorial down the road. Morning classes are compulsory – the 'Summer School', as its name implies, is educational and that is part of the contract with the University of St Andrews. But the participants are keen to learn – whether they are beginners or children or youths attending courses geared for them (in Week Three), or intermediates like myself, or experts like Charly Candia wanting to improve their dancing over any of the four weeks of 'school'.

Sue Porter, the School Director, explains that at the first class of the week the teachers will observe how people dance and decide if anyone should go up or down. Of course, they have to be very polite asking someone to shift to a lower class – from, say, a 'High Impact' advanced class to one for

Summer School dancers in 'double triangles' in the Younger Hall, St Andrews

'Essential Skills'. The tutor cannot demand that a student changes class from the one they themselves nominated. However, most individuals realise that any proposed transfer is for their own benefit.

In the afternoon there are optional activities: Scottish Step (a soft-shoe variety), choreography workshops and 'personal feedback'. I tended to go sightseeing or swimming in the sea after lunch but signed up for one 'personal feedback' where an immaculate French dancing master scrutinised the footwork of a dozen of us from the intermediate class. We were all found wanting – though one woman did a *Pas de Basque* which earned a 'Not bad' from the tutor!

All the teachers home in on neat steps, upright deportment and correct hand-holds – details that reelers would find tiresome but which make for graceful dancing. The greatest challenge for me, though, was the sheer number of dances and the complexity of many of them. Apart from the two or three we learnt every morning, there were about 40 more on the combined programmes of the evening parties. I knew only six of those. The rest had unfamiliar names and several were very tricky – highlighted by three crowns on the list of dances. Amongst those were 'The Aviator', 'MacDonald of Keppoch' and 'Quarries Jig'. Fortunately, the Younger Hall has balconies from which less proficient dancers like me could watch the skilful exponents sprint through the 'Three Crown' dances.

Sue Porter took everything in her stride. She was taught by Jean Milligan and has been coming to St Andrews since 1972 when everyone dressed more formally and the Lumsden

Wing, which now accommodates all and sundry, was off limits to men and known as 'The Nunnery'!

It is not just old hands, like Sue, who are experts. I was equally impressed by Aya Ito, a young Japanese woman who started Scottish dancing in Tokyo in 2017 and is now in the top class at St Andrews. She appreciates the concentrated tuition day after day and the opportunity to partner other skilful dancers. One such is Arthur Baum, a handsome American who first danced in Los Angeles and now continues where he lives in North Carolina, as well as attending summer dance camps elsewhere in the States and at the mecca for all Scottish Country Dancers: St Andrews. Arthur is a physicist and he befriended two other like-minded young dancers in the advanced class – Juliane Dannberg from Germany and Emily Filmer from Adelaide, Australia. All three work in scientific, technical spheres and they reckon that helps them pick up and memorise the patterns of a dance. For the experienced students, those dances might encompass a fiendish mix of moves and formations called 'Bourrel', 'Espagnole', 'Spoke', 'Targe', 'Tourbillon'...

In the intermediate class I was hard pressed mastering the simpler 'Knot' and 'Set and Link for Three'. But we all enjoyed the process and the camaraderie. I made friends with a married couple from Australia – Karen Haig and Mark Muggeridge. Karen was a student at St Andrews, so she at least knows the town, if not all the dances we encountered that week. She and her husband live in Sydney in an old colonial part called the Rocks – hence the name for their group of twenty or so dancers, 'Scots on the Rocks'!

North Carolina resident, Arthur Baum, with a Scottish Country Dancing partner

Karen Haig and Mark Muggeridge from Sydney at a 'Chaotic Ceilidh'

Having travelled so far, the couple were incorporating their week in St Andrews into a whole holiday visiting friends, relatives and other parts of Europe. Likewise, two sisters from New Zealand, Isabel Jackson and Barbara Laing, were making the most of their time away from home with Summer School as the highlight. They admitted to being quite star-struck dancing and dining beside tutors and musicians they had seen for years on the RSCDS website and YouTube.

Many of the participants I spoke to had first danced at ceilidhs. Thankfully there was ceilidh dancing one evening which gave our brains a rest as the dances are so easy. There was also the other sort of ceilidh where we sat around a hall, the swiftly assembled choir sang two Scottish songs, others did their party pieces (dancing or acting), the then RSCDS chairman, William Williamson, directed proceedings and sang some solos, having a strong tenor voice. But on most evenings the entertainment was Scottish Country Dancing, both informal in the Common Room or with people dressed up at the Younger Hall.

The grand finale on the Saturday night started with 'The Shetland Shepherdess' which I had no idea how to do. Luckily, I was shepherded onto the floor by a charming man who danced superbly. It transpired he was Gary Coull, chairman-elect of the RSCDS – the ideal person to follow in the footsteps of William Williamson.

I danced also with Mark from 'Scots on the Rocks'. I asked Mark if he minded being in the minority as a man at Summer School (since there are so many more women than men). 'No,' he replied, 'It means I never get to dance

Gary Coull & William Williamson in 2023 celebrating 100th anniversary of RSCDS and the Flying Scotsman train
Photo: Jon Davey

on the women's side which keeps it simple. Karen has to switch and is often dancing as a man.' I wondered what his Australian mates think of his hobby. 'Well, I love telling them our holiday plans – that we're going to "school" for a week of Scottish dancing. You should see their jaws drop!'

Peter Knight, who wrote the Collins Pocket Reference book on Scottish country dancing (in 1996), started dancing aged nine at his Hemel Hempstead school. He is English through and through having been born in Kent. But, as a boy, he went to Scotland on holiday with his parents, liked the dancing and carried on with it as an adult in Oxted, Surrey. He currently lives with his partner, Margaret Shaw, in London where he's taught Scottish dancing at Wandsworth

Old friends Peter Knight and Gilly Nester-Smith

Town Hall and at the Little Ship Club, formerly in Blackfriars, now at Pont Street. He's also taught in Scotland, including on the Isle of Mull where one Scotsman was amazed to find an Englishman who knew so many Scottish dances and was teaching them to less accomplished Scots.

As a teacher Peter is quite strict. Like thousands of others down south, I learnt from classes with Peter and well remember his bark (worse than his bite): 'DON'T TWIZZLE!' – just keep going in the direction of travel. When couples turn each other or spin he prefers the 'elbow grip' rather than grabbing each other by the hand. He has witnessed several injuries: two men concussing each other during a Foursome Reel at Oban, a girl breaking an arm at the Perth Ball. At a club in London Peter said to one man, 'Don't hold your partner like that because if you slip, you'll break her thumb.' 'Well,' came the reply, 'that will be her fault!' In recalling that incident Peter added darkly, 'You get people like that.'

Apart from a few arrogant types, his most challenging pupils are those with no sense of rhythm and the uncoordinated. 'Some people,' says Peter, 'simply don't know left from right. I quite understand why driving instructors might tell a client to put an L and R on their hands before a test!'

Peter regularly teaches both reelers (who he calls 'Hard Shoes') and Scottish Country Dancers ('Soft Shoes'). He himself wears the traditional leather ghillie slipper (with laces) and a kilt, and prefers SCD primarily for its range of dances. He reckons reelers are limited to ten favourites because they don't know the formations, the building blocks for all dances. He recalls one occasion when he was teaching some young Londoners at Pont Street and he said, 'Hands up all of you who know 'The Duke of Perth'?' All raised their hands. 'Hands up all of you who know what I mean by "corner, partner, corner, partner"?' Nobody did. 'The reelers,' he continues, 'are taught the whole pattern not the parts of it.' He himself would get bored doing the same ten reels over and over again. 'I remember one Caledonian Ball where the band played 'The Duke of Perth' 14 times! I counted. Everybody claps and stamps and they do it yet again. Unbelievable!'

He concedes, though, that the 'pointy toe brigade', Scottish Country Dancers, could not last the course doing neat *Pas de Basque* with a *jeté* or leap for the length of a reeling ball. 'If you're dancing all night till 3.00am, no way can you do proper *Pas de Basque* so there's some sense in it – shuffling like the reelers.'

I queried how women, in particular, are meant to move. According to the reelers' *Swinging Sporran* manual, 'A lady should give the impression she is moving round on wheels. It is considered unladylike to bounce'. So, what does Peter Knight think of the idea that women should glide? 'It's nonsense. Women can dance as they like and tend to leap higher because they've done ballet.'

In his ninth decade, Peter appears to be less of a stickler. Whilst his greatest delight is Scottish Country Dancing and teaching it, he sees the appeal and merit of every genre. 'It's all fine,' he concludes, 'but ladies should never raise their arms in a ballroom!'

CHAPTER FOUR

Reeling and Reelers

THE IMPETUS FOR reelers differs from that of Scottish Country Dancers. Dedicated reelers do not want to practise and perfect their dancing at weekly classes. They usually attend just one or two events a year where the dances are familiar ones so they don't have to worry about where to move or who to spin. They know the form – and some formations – and socialising is as important as the dancing.

Even so, the dances have to be learnt. Older reelers might recall going to Miss Matthew's classes in Elgin or Mrs Grant's in Dingwall whilst Londoners flocked to Veronica Maitland Makgill Crichton's (until 1966) and, from 1971 for decades, the Wandsworth Reels run by Harry Verney and Elisabeth Colquhoun. Today, the London Reels in the capital and Stockbridge Reelers in Edinburgh are hugely popular, teaching people who have not learnt either at school or from their parents the ten key dances that will feature at a reeling ball.

Those dances are as follows:

'The Dashing White Sergeant'
'The Eightsome Reel'
'The Foursome'
'Mairi's Wedding'
'Hamilton House'

'Machine without Horses'
'The Duke of Perth'
'Inverness Country Dance' (or 'Speed the Plough')
'The Duke and Duchess of Edinburgh'
'The Reel of the 51st Division'

Confusingly, only the first three listed above are proper reels, which are danced in a ring and which feature 'reels of three' (or four) where dancers interweave making figures of eight. The remaining seven are country dances arranged in long sets and named after the tunes to which they were originally danced.

Enthusiastic reelers preparing for a spin
Photo: Flora Wilson

For people unable to attend live classes there are several useful YouTube videos of the individual dances. But before the advent of the internet, the crucial instruction manual was – and still is – *The Swinging Sporran.* Two friends, Roddy Martine and Andrew Campbell, back in the 1970s, saw a gap in the market for a simple guide to the main dances listed time and again at parties. They were not interested in most of the *101 Scottish Country Dances* that the RSCDS had published (in 1956). So, they jointly wrote and illustrated the amusing *Swinging Sporran* with clear directions on the ten key numbers plus a few more, along with historical notes and guidance on dress. In the earlier editions there is also a hilarious description of The Scottish Season – 'a kind of keep-fit course held in late August and early September.'

Correct

I talked to both authors at their homes: Roddy in Edinburgh, Andrew in Somerset, England. Over 50 years on from when their book was first published, in 1973, they are tall and sprightly, a testament to their life-long enthusiasm for reeling.

Even as a boy Roddy often drew 'doodles and diagrams' as he put it. He credits Andy, 'a Highland boy', with better knowledge of Scottish dances. Thus, Andy wrote the instructions for *The Swinging Sporran* reels whilst Roddy covered the history and concentrated on the drawings. The booklet aimed to be

Roddy Martine, co-author of *The Swinging Sporran*, in earlier days light-hearted and the depictions undoubtedly are. All the female dancers are pouting and haughty, the men keen and frisky.

The working title was 'The Reel Thing'. But, as Roddy explained, 'We were worried people might think it was about fishing so we changed the name.' In the 1980s the word 'reel' gained prominence in an *Observer* magazine article by Jean Birney – 'Reel Scots and Real Scots'. She and a photographer gate-crashed the Skye Ball and her resulting piece focused on the difference between real Scottish people and the posh Anglo-Scots who reeled. Roddy reckons the social divide lingers on to this day but less so.

He has danced with all sorts and everywhere: alongside the Royal Family at Preston Hall near Edinburgh, partnering the Duchess of Argyll at one Caledonian Ball and attending Tartan Week in the USA. 'I was once in Atlanta,' said Roddy, 'and this woman came up to me in my kilt and exclaimed, "Oh I love you Scottish people. You're so poor!" I didn't know what to say. She obviously had a vision of a tiny croft in the Highlands.' He was equally nonplussed when berated by a red-faced general, covered in braid, for apparently casting off incorrectly in 'The Machine without Horses'. 'You should get a book called *The Swinging Sporran*,' boomed the general, 'and damn well learn to dance!'

Whilst Roddy never purported to be an expert reeler, Andrew Campbell definitely is. He learnt to dance at the age of five at Mrs Grant's in Dingwall then carried on at school, university, attending balls at Donside, Deeside, the Caledonian and Skye. It was, for him, quite straightforward, therefore, explaining the basic steps and formations in a handy little book.

Even so, he acknowledges getting one thing wrong when he instructed women doing 'The Foursome' to start by passing each other right shoulder to right shoulder when traditionally they pass with left shoulders in the centre. The guidance is otherwise spot on and particularly useful for people wanting to reel since it also explains the Aberdonian style which reelers favour and which involves everyone dancing the whole length of a set simultaneously. As *The Swinging Sporran* warns, there is 'no time for inattention, sleeping or gossiping' in, for instance, 'The Reel of the 51st Division' danced as an Aberdonian.

Helicopters – a challenging formation where the men sweep the women off their feet, on this occasion at the Perth Ball

Courtesy of Perth Ball and *Scottish Field*, photographer Angus Blackburn

Other aspects of reeling that make it exceptionally energetic are the spins whereby partners swing each other around. The more athletic ones in 'The Foursome' also do 'helicopters' – the two men lifting their partners and wheeling them around so the women are literally swept off their feet. Andy Campbell, who has often danced in this way until dawn, sets great store on wooden floors, ideally, sprung. He went reeling at a beautiful palace in Venice but the floor was made of stone – 'awful on the knees'. He also values good lighting – 'You need to be able to see your partner's eyes, partly to anticipate their moves.' Like most men who dance he is chivalrous, ushering his female partner to wherever she should be and steadying her after a spin. He disapproves of the recent trend

Andy Campbell seeing eye to eye with his dance partner, Cindy Gray
Photo courtesy of of Dena Woodhams

of young men swinging their partners clockwise and anti-clockwise – 'I think it jolts the rhythm and flow of the dance.'

However one birls or spins, it requires skill and that, for Andy, is the appeal of reeling. 'Getting good at something is satisfying,' he elaborates, 'and so much more fun than, say, a rowing machine.' As for balls, they hold a special attraction for men giving them a rare opportunity to dress up 'in colourful stuff like kilts' and then dance with eight or so women in the space of ten minutes. He followed what he describes as the usual pattern. 'You reel a lot when you're courting, then more to cement the relationship, you stop when you're busy with children, then revert to it when you're older.' The Campbells' five children all reel. 'It's a fantastic way to mix in a non-threatening way.'

Andy is often a steward at parties, helping guests get into sets. One of his most challenging assignments was in Aviemore organising an Eightsome writ large – a '128 some' – with Prince Charles as one of the reelers. Amongst the regular reels he cites 'Mairi's Wedding' as the trickiest as, 'You can't give your partner a helping hand. Everyone in the eight has to know what they are doing and where they are going.'

As both Andrew Campbell and Roddy Martine acknowledge in *The Swinging Sporran*, there is invariably 'the person who has done one or two dances under pressure and who always feels completely lost.' Their book is aimed at just such individuals enabling them to 'hold their own by diligent use of the following pages'. Those pages are now in their 14th edition, much to the delight of the pair who wrote them and the legions of dancers who have benefited from them.

The Verneys at St Columba's Church, Pont Street, London, geared up for dancing

Another man who stands tall in reeling circles is Harry Verney. For decades he organised the Wandsworth Reels, later moving from the town hall in Wandsworth to the larger one in Hammersmith for a St Andrew's Ball and the more central London location of St Columba's church hall for regular sessions.

Harry himself is Scottish and wears a Cawdor-Campbell tartan as he is descended from the Earl of Cawdor and the Campbells of Nairn who, he assured me, 'are very different from the bad Campbells who murdered everybody!' He was brought up, though, in London where he went to Madame Vacani's off the Brompton Road for dancing lessons. He learnt 'The Eightsome', which he did at a few hunt balls, sometimes sabotaged by anti-hunt protesters who let down car tyres while the owners were dancing.

Once, when he was 28, a group of girls approached him saying they were a man short for a dance. He admitted he knew only 'The Eightsome' but they persuaded him to join them regardless. That was the start of a lifelong interest in reels which he mastered at sessions run by Veronica Maitland Makgill Crichton, subsequently perfecting them at Twickenham Boat Club balls.

When Veronica stopped organising reels in 1966, Harry saw an opportunity to establish them on a larger scale. But, being disorganised, he recognised the need for an efficient, competent person to book venues and help on administration. The perfect candidate was an acquaintance, Elisabeth Colquhoun (née Stanning) who duly came on board, booking the first space, Wandsworth Town Hall, in 1971.

The monthly Wandsworth Reels swiftly became extremely popular. The hall had a capacity for 500 people – though 300 dancers was a sensible number – but many more turned up. When 650 would-be reelers came along, 150 of them had to queue outside, waiting to enter if anyone left early. Thereafter Harry and Elisabeth instituted a booking system with vouchers.

The music initially was vinyl records with a DJ. Later there was live music from Frank Reid and his band. Both Harry and Elisabeth would instruct, sticking to the ten main reels plus 'Posties Jig'. 'Gate money' was 'about 50p' and any profits were donated to charities like The Guide Dogs for the Blind Association. The participants were mainly young people, though middle-aged ones sometimes attended – notably, Princess Margaret and her friends. They, too, were 'a man short' so Harry Verney stepped into the breach.

In association with Wandsworth Reels, Harry and Elisabeth also organised triumphant balls in the Great Room of the Grosvenor House Hotel. They needed to sell 800 tickets to break even (as the venue is expensive) but managed to do so easily. One year they mustered 1,000 guests, with a further 250 arriving at midnight. Harry recalls how wonderful it was 'seeing hundreds of reelers spinning in a line all the way down the ballroom floor.'

Like several others, Harry met the woman he was to marry at Wandsworth Reels. In 2021, at the 50th anniversary of the association, they asked couples to raise their hands if they had met at Wandsworth Reels and 'lots went up'. As people get older they tend to leave London and settle in other places in the UK, taking reeling with them. Harry, for instance, on becoming a family man, moved to Winchester, where he arranged dances with picnics for up to 250 people, aged nine to 90. 'We had the simple dances first and the more complicated ones like 'Machine without Horses' after midnight, by which time the little children had disappeared.'

As with the Verneys, the Colquhouns (Elisabeth and her husband Alastair) passed their enthusiasm for reeling on to their children. The Colquhouns' son, Andrew, together with his cousin Robert, even devised a dance, the 'Kandahar Reel' as a tribute to their fallen comrades, fellow Black Watch soldiers on duty in Afghanistan in 2009. Two groups of four dancers join hands across, symbolising the twin blades of the Chinook helicopter in use at the time.

Elisabeth Colquhoun , dance tutor and former co-organiser of the Wandsworth Reels

The fast moving 'Kandahar Reel' is one of dozens that Elisabeth Colquhoun knows and has taught. She likes both reeling and Scottish Country Dancing having learnt the steps and formations from the age of 11 when she was living in New Zealand. Decades later, working as a school teacher in London, Elisabeth also became a proficient dance tutor. She strives to encourage both old and young dancers. She recalls Christmas holiday sessions for children and teenagers: 'We'd always finish with 'The Dashing White Sergeant'. Parents came to collect with their little ones in tow, who took to the floor. So did teenagers who had actually come to mock their friends. We'd persuade them to make up numbers. They joined in, loved it and asked to come back!'

She played a crucial role in the smooth running of the Wandsworth Reels. 'Harry was the MC,' she explained, 'and bought the orange squash. I did everything else – for instance, in the early years, booking the DJs, including Bruce Williams and Richard Duxbury.' On the occasion when Princess Margaret, Roddy Llewellyn and friends turned up (early), the DJ, Richard, had popped across to the pub for a sandwich so there was no music playing. The royal party rushed onto the stage clamouring for 'Music! Music!' and started to move the grand piano which was strictly forbidden. Thankfully, the DJ returned, put on a record and Elisabeth and Harry soon had everyone on the floor.

They are justifiably proud of the funds they raised for charity, notably the purchase of Sergeant, Gay, Gordon, Duchess, Hamilton, Duke, Inverness, Mairi, Trust, Andrew and Davey as guide dogs for the blind. Elisabeth is also pleased

John Carver of the London Reels, which carried on from the Wandsworth Reels as set up by Harry Verney (on the right)
Photo: Emma Sutton

that Wandsworth Reels lives on – renamed as London Reels and galvanised by John Carver.

John was already an adult when he started reeling in London near Parsons Green Tube – or 'PGT' as it's generally known. 'I was terrified the first time,' he admits, 'but there was a welcoming crowd, a good pub next door and I enjoyed those PGTs more and more as I came to learn the dances.' He carried on at London Reels (formerly Wandsworth Reels), now at Pont Street, eventually running the whole show and teaching the reels with panache.

'We have new people coming in all the time. Most are in their 20s and 30s but some seasoned dancers who are going to the Caledonian Ball or a highland one (and who haven't reeled for ages) come along to remind themselves.' John has the evening practices down to a fine art. 'We have committee members partner newcomers and they help sets that are struggling. Experienced dancers do a demonstration of the next reel. Everyone watches that. Then we all do a walk through before having a go with music.' John gives guidance on two-handed holds and the overhead turn. He notes that, 'Some novices just throw the lady like a frisbee hoping she'll end up in the right place. We encourage the man to hold onto the lady until the end of a spin, placing her where she needs to be next.'

London Reels tend to have a fairly even mix of men and women, but John prefers to have too many women rather than too many men as men are less willing to dance with each other. 'A woman is usually much happier to volunteer to be "an honorary man".' There is no shortage of customers. Over the last seven years there's been a steady 20 per cent increase annually. 'We used to have about 140 people. Now over 300 come to a typical session.' Less than 10 per cent of them are Scots. 'But isn't that great?' says John cheerfully, 'Scottish dancing is one of Scotland's greatest exports.'

A notable achievement of John's was creating tutorial videos of the core reels. Having worked as an IT teacher at a boys' prep school in Oxfordshire, he realised how powerful

London Reels tutorial video with arrows pointing to 1st and 2nd 'corners'

video could be for learning. Books like *The Swinging Sporran* were, for him, an excellent starting point but, as he says, 'Video can bring diagrams to life with music, timing, rhythm, to say nothing of the joys of using slow motion to understand the main teaching points.' So, from 2015 onwards John organised demonstrations – using his best dancers at London Reels – which he filmed and carefully edited, superimposing arrows, graphics and acronyms, with each video being under five minutes long to ensure they were digestible. Those videos, now on YouTube, are watched by millions of viewers. John was chuffed to hear from a primary school teacher in Tahiti who used the tutorials to teach her class how to reel on the beach!

After eight years in charge of London Reels, John recently stepped down and members of his committee now deal with social media and take it in turns to teach. Following John's lead, London Reels remains in good hands decades after the era when it was in Wandsworth and dancers sent stamped, addressed envelopes to Elisabeth Colquhoun in return for entry vouchers. People now pay mainly by credit card for the practices and online for ball tickets, which are speedily snapped up.

The London Reels 2022 ball coincided with the one-year anniversary of the invasion of Ukraine so half the profits from the £59 per person tickets went to British-Ukrainian Aid, the other half going to Blood Bikes Scotland, which ferries reserves of blood across the Highlands. The 2024 ball raised over £10,000 for other worthwhile causes. Raising money for charity, enshrined by Wandsworth Reels, carries

Energetic reelers at Battersea Arts Centre
Photo: Flora Wilson

on at London Reels as steered by John Carver and now his crew.

Inspired in part by the London Reels, Peter MacDonald in Edinburgh has been running a similar reeling group in Stockbridge in the centre of the city. It recently celebrated its tenth anniversary. About 90 people start in January when there is a six-week beginners' course and more experienced reelers can come for free to help out. During the rest of the year the usual turn out is around 60 (half men, half women). Everyone is welcome and there is a walk-through of each dance.

Apart from the standard ten reels, the Stockbridge repertoire includes 'The Gay Gordons' and, because of Peter's previous military career, the challenging 'Kandahar Reel'. The venue is the Life Care Centre, to which they donate any surplus from the sessions (at £5 per person). It is very much a community enterprise with people from all walks of life, primarily from Stockbridge but also from further afield. There are quite a few young professionals: a ship's architect, a female airline pilot… Peter, whose parents were keen Scottish dancers, teaches the reels while Jo Leitch does the administration. Together they also organise two big ceilidhs (in May and December) with a live band, 'Clappy Do', and a dress code of 'Highland Casual' such as a kilt and open necked shirt.

Whilst most of the Scottish universities, including Edinburgh, have thriving reeling societies, the Stockbridge Reelers is a magnet for people other than students who want to carry on reeling. Peter is drawn to the stirring music and likes the simplicity of reels which means he can do all the dances without feeling self-conscious. Another Stockbridge regular cites reeling as the single constant in his life. 'I've got dance cards from balls and parties going back 50 years. I just love it. It generates endorphins and gives you a lot of satisfaction.'

CHAPTER FIVE

Balls

HIGHLIGHTED ON ANY Scottish dancer's calendar is the ball – or balls if you have the energy and funds for more than one. Over the years I've been to Scottish Country Dancing balls from Blair Atholl to Wimbledon; reeling ones like the Royal Caledonian in London and the Northern Meeting near Inverness as well as reels abroad in the Palace of Versailles and in Oman. I've arranged St Andrew's Day and Burns Night balls at the Hurlingham Club where we do a mix of SCD and reeling. For St Andrew's Day there may be blue and white candles or table linen in keeping with Scotland's Saltire flag since St Andrew is the patron saint of Scotland (with his feast day in November). At Burns Night there are several rituals: the piping in of a haggis, a dramatic skewering of it, 'The Immortal Memory' (a speech celebrating the life of Scotland's bard, Robert Burns) and toasts to the lassies and laddies.

Everyone dresses up. The men in kilts or tartan trews vie with the women in colourful silk dresses. There is, invariably, a live band which galvanizes the dancers. The venues are usually grand and spacious – large enough for scores of people and vigorous spinning.There are weird quirks like dance cards with tiny pencils on a string and an adherence to traditions: you go in a group where the men invite all

British reelers en route to Versailles Ball in May 2022

the women 'on their table' for a dance (duly scribbled onto the dance cards) and can only seek other partners once this obligation is fulfilled. At the reeling balls, where there are 'carriages' at dawn, there is usually breakfast served after midnight with kedgeree on the menu. The whole party ends with all the guests joining hands in a huge circle, singing 'Auld Lang Syne' and the National Anthem, then pairing up again to gallop around doing a polka.

One of the most impressive ballrooms is at Blair Castle.

Piping in the haggis at a Burns Night ball
Photo: Isobel McTear

Baronial in style, it was completed by the 7th Duke of Atholl in 1876 and displays a portrait, by Sir Henry Raeburn, of composer and musician Niel Gow along with his famous fiddle. The walls are festooned with antlers, as are the corridors leading to the main room. I went to Blair Castle for an Aberfeldy Ball, held annually before Christmas, with a mix of SCD and the standard reels. Proceedings start with a Grand March. Couples line up in the corridor, approach the ballroom and walk to the end of it where an MC directs

The 2016 ball in Florence at the Palazzo Vecchio (as old and palatial as its name)
Photo courtesy of Dena Woodhams

Space for a spin, thanks to the large venue
Photo courtesy of Dena Woodhams

every pair to veer left or right back towards the entrance doors. Each pair then joins with another so four at a time proceed down the room and are again waved left or right. Foursomes join up so that rows of eight pace down the room to be directed into spaces ready for 'The Eightsome Reel'. It's a nifty way to mix people up and to organise sets speedily.

The origins of the Royal Caledonian Ball go back to 1822, when the Duke and Duchess of Atholl hosted the 'Grand Caledonian Ball' at Almack's Assembly Rooms in Mayfair, London. It was held in aid of the Caledonian Asylum, an institution launched in 1815 by members of the Highland Society of London to provide a home and education for Scottish children who had been orphaned during the Napoleonic Wars. The 1822 ball, which attracted some 1,200

Filling in dance cards, a traditional ritual before a ball begins
Photo: Flora Wilson

'Auld Lang Syne' finale at a London Reels ball
Photo: Flora Wilson

people, took place months before King George IV's visit to Scotland during the 'Tartan Revival'. The ball continued annually, receiving Royal Patronage in 1841 – though members of the extended Royal Family had by that point attended the Ball for several years already. It first became known as the Royal Caledonian Ball in 1851.

Today, the Royal Caledonian Ball starts with 'set reels'. Twelve groups headed by the Chairman, the Organiser, army captains and patrons proceed onto the floor in a prearranged order, each to a specific space on the Grosvenor House ballroom floor, for the first Eightsomes and Sixteensomes. The remaining 600 or so dancers look on, biding their time until everyone heads to the floor for several hours of energetic reels. I was in the 'set reels' in 2025 but only because I fitted the bill: I wore a tartan sash, had a partner in a kilt and had been invited by one of the patronesses, Marina Arkell. There are about 150 patronesses (including several Ladies and 'Hons') whose role may have stemmed from the Directresses of the 19th-century Assemblies who also had to ensure that the dancers appeared in proper attire.

Another patroness at the Royal Caledonian Ball is Sue Dawson, who admits that the women's key role is to raise money. Since it started in 1822, the ball has always supported charities, initially the Caledonian Asylum, more recently a wide range of Scottish concerns – for instance, Riding for the Disabled in Glasgow. In return for bringing guests and getting donations or raffle prizes, Sue and other patronesses attending the ball have preferential treatment, being seated at the best end of the ballroom (formerly an ice rink) and being entitled to join the set reels which her husband, Guy, has often arranged.

Guy is on the executive committee headed by the Earl of Kinnoull and the Earl of Errol and chaired by John Shields. It was they who had to cope with a disaster in 2018 when the floor collapsed resulting in the ball being disbanded, despite the Scots Guards and other soldiers amongst the guests offering to mend it. The Scots Guards in their red and gold uniforms have long been a colourful cohort at the Grosvenor House balls, and many a lass has fallen for the glamour of a major or captain who can reel. Alannah Mcdonald, for example, met the man she was to marry, Lieutenant Colonel Andrew Speed, at a Royal Caledonian Ball. One of the couple's favourite dances is 'The Reel of the 51st Division', devised by three highland officers in a prisoner of war camp in Germany in 1940.

Far removed from the military and the exigencies of war, Guy and Sue Dawson describe themselves as 'lifestyle reelers'. Whilst their friends might go to the gym, the Dawsons choose to reel. As well as being stalwarts of the Royal Caledonian, they also regularly attend the balls in Oban and Skye. The gathering at Skye started in the Victorian era and notably came to public attention in August 2008 when an article in the *Daily Record* described 'Posh ball mayhem as gatecrasher headbutts laird's son'! Apparently a 34-year-old unemployed fisherman turned up at 4.00am claiming to be a clan chief. He then accused the organiser, 'Loon' cartoonist Sir Alasdair Hilleary, of being 'f*** English'. The case went to court where Andrew Murphy, defending, asked, 'Are they still hooting and hurraying at 4.00am?' Hilleary replied, 'Yes. They are still enjoying themselves dancing the Highland reels and jigs in a beautiful, formal, elegant manner.' I wish I'd been a fly (or midge) on the wall both at that Skye Ball and the court room thereafter!

Another reeler who (unlike Alasdair Hilleary) is English through and through is Anne Glenconner, former Lady in Waiting to Princess Margaret. Lady Glenconner told me how she learnt to reel – and do the Sword Dance – from the age of five with her Ogilvy cousins. From her teens she went to the Perth Ball, where on one occasion the charm bracelet she was

Dashing Scots Guards amongst the guests at a Royal Caledonian ball
Photo: Dafydd Jones

Anne, Baroness Glenconner (née Coke)
National Portrait Gallery. Photo: Navana Vandyk

wearing got caught in the tartan of her partner, David Airlie. Abandoning the set was not an option. Mercifully, Anne's aunt was standing by, came to the rescue and disentangled them.

Of all the Highland balls, the most venerable is the Northern Meeting which started in 1788. Its stated object was 'Pleasure and Innocent Amusement' and its purpose was to promote 'a Social Intercourse between Families of Ladies and Gentlemen of the Northern Counties'. To make it less elitist the Northern Meeting used to include horse racing, tugs of war, tossing the caber and piping competitions. Now only the piping and dancing continue, but the organisation has latterly revived popular approval by raising money for community projects – for example, a new hut for a hockey club in the Highlands. Also, the balls are no longer exclusively for Northern grandees – outsiders can attend provided Northern Meeting members vouch for them. I was fortunate in being invited to the 2023 ball by the then Convenor of the Northern Meeting, Bridie Graham, whose father, Alan Cameron, had also been a convenor.

Like so many who live near Inverness where the Northern Meeting was originally held, Bridie learnt to dance at Mrs Grant's in Dingwall. She has reeled all her life, falling in love with her husband, Donald, when they first danced 'The Duke of Perth'. She has been to many Northern Meeting balls including the impressive Bicentenary one held at Beaufort Castle. The quest for venues is a constant problem. Derelict castles, hotels, halls, an ice rink, a spa pavilion and a redundant lunatic asylum have all been mooted. But as the Northern Meeting needs rooms for less than one week a year

Lady Graham (Bridie) in a skirt made of her family tartans, ready for the Picnic Ball at the end of the Northern Meeting nothing is financially viable. However, Bridie was pleased to have secured Fort George for the 2023 ball which I attended.

The fort is just across the water from the Black Isle (where the Grahams live and where we dined beforehand). The edifice looks impregnable, with ramparts, moats and wooden palings, but for the Northern Meeting it appeared to be welcoming, lit up with pink and yellow lights leading to two huge marquees – one for 'breakfast' and one for dancing. From 10.15 until 5.00am, 360 dancers took to the floor for the 20 dances on the programme – mostly reels with some foxtrots and quicksteps in between – played with gusto by the Pictish Players. Everyone looked their best: the young women in slinky dresses, the men in kilts or White Tie with a mix, as Bridie put it, of 'old codgers and codgeresses doing the '*Pas de Basque*' alongside the uninhibited rutting of the young who, for instance, don't do the St Andrew's cross, balancing in line during 'The Reel of the 51st', because they're so busy spinning.'

Amongst the guests was a Rod Stewart lookalike who turned out to be Peregrine Moncreiffe of that Ilk, 2nd son of Sir Iain Moncreiffe who used to partner Queen Elizabeth at Scottish balls. There were also scores of Frasers. I was amused to hear an exchange between two teenage girls: 'By the way, I'm NOT a Fraser.' 'Well I never, I'm not either!'

Their younger siblings were looking forward to the Picnic Ball the following evening. This more informal event, started in the 1980s, is open to members and friends aged nine to 90, though Bridie confessed that her own mother snuck in aged 91 – 'very illegal'! She relishes seeing different generations dancing together, mirroring her own enthusiasm. 'I've always

Fort George, moats and ramparts leading to the main edifice
Visit Scotland. Photo: Colin Keldie

Youths spinning, leaving 'balancing in line' to the older brigade
Photo: Isobel McTear

Queen Elizabeth II and Sir Iain Moncreiffe of that Ilk – regular partners at Scottish balls

RSCDS and Scotsman Publications, 1973

loved reeling. It's healthy, good exercise. At the end of the evening my throat is dry, not from whooping but because I sing the tunes as I dance all the way down.'

The convenors of the Northern Meeting are always invited to the annual Piping Competition where Bridie is again in her element since her husband, Graham, plays the bagpipes (as

Alastair Campbell (left), Dena Woodhams (centre) and Mark Tennant (right) – three of the Pinstripe Highlanders

Photo courtesy of Dena Woodhams

did her father). Another piper and former Convenor of the Northern Meeting is Mark Tennant who was instrumental in arranging six glorious balls abroad.

Mark Tennant started reeling at Miss Matthew's dancing class in Elgin but was thrown out, aged four, for 'snogging' the cobbler's daughter – also aged four! He carried on regardless, dancing at school and becoming a proficient reeler and bagpiper. In 2000 the Caledonian Society of St Petersburg invited the Skye Gathering to a ball in the

Shuvalov Palace. As the then Convenor of the Northern Meeting, Mark was a guest at the St Petersburg ball and was inspired by it to hold his own organisation's ball in an unusual setting. Vienna, the quintessential home of balls, seemed the obvious choice.

However, Mark had no associates in Vienna nor any knowledge of the language nor how to set about organising a ball abroad. But he knew just the person to fix everything: a multi-lingual American woman, Andrena Woodhams, who, like Mark, played the bagpipes in the Pinstripe Highlanders band. She is savvy and capable, and was living in Vienna at the time. Mark rang Dena (her preferred name) and asked if she could give him any tips. 'I won't give you tips,' came the reply. 'I'll organise it.'

Dena contacted John McGregor, British ambassador for Austria, who readily came on board. He offered his residence for the ball which took place in 2006 with 220 Highlanders reeling and Austrians in dirndls waltzing in at half time.

Buoyed by the success of Vienna, the Mark and Dena duo sought more foreign fields. Peter Forrester of the Argyllshire Gathering joined them, making a trio to create the next ball in Venice in 2009, with help from Donata Grimani. The numbers of guests had doubled to 440, who arrived at the venue, the Palazzo Donà dalle Rose, in 80 gondolas with every sixth gondola carrying a piper at the stern. Amongst them were Donald Graham and Mark Tennant, who told me how difficult it is playing the bagpipes standing on a wobbly gondola and having to stoop under the bridges. 'At the Rialto,' Mark recalls, 'the Japanese tourists were going

Dena Woodhams, Peter Forrester, Donata Grimani and Mark Tennant in Venice, 2009

Photo courtesy of Dena Woodhams

Bagpiper on gondola in Venice on the way to the Palazzo Donà dalle Rose for a ball

Photo courtesy of Dena Woodhams

Ciragan Palace Hotel, Istanbul, venue for an international gathering of reelers in 2012
Photo courtesy of Dena Woodhams

bananas, click, click, clicking their cameras as Scottish airs wafted over Venice from us bagpipers in kilts!' En route to Italy, several guests who had travelled there on the Orient Express danced Foursomes to the pipes at Innsbruck Station, much to the astonishment of train staff and passengers.

It was not only Scots who travelled to the next ball abroad. By 2012, when Mark and Dena had secured the Ciragan Palace Hotel in Istanbul as a venue, 700 people from 17 different countries arrived in Turkey in order to dance. All went swimmingly – apart from some actual swimmers, young reelers who had stripped off and were bathing at 4.00am in the hotel pool by the Bosphorus in full view of passing sailors. Mark had to apologise to the Turkish manager explaining that 'reeling is so hot'. 'Yes, I understand why

Making friends

Photo courtesy of Dena Woodhams

Above: Pre-ball entertainment in Jaipur, India, in March 2014
Below: Maharajah of Jodhpur at the 'Blue Ball', March 2014
Photos courtesy of Dena Woodhams

Indian extravaganza, March 2014
Photo courtesy of Dena Woodhams

Reelers in India, March 2014
Photo courtesy of Dena Woodhams

Reelers at Palazzo Vecchio in 2016
Photo courtesy of Dena Woodhams

The younger contingent
Photo courtesy of Dena Woodhams

Guests gathered at the Royal Opera House in Muscat, Oman, 1 November 2018
Photo courtesy of Dena Woodhams

they did it,' the hotelier replied, 'but not in front of the river in a floodlit garden!'

The next foray was even more exotic. Tennant had set his heart on India. Dena, always up for a challenge, contacted the Maharajah of Jodhpur securing his fort for a 'Blue Ball', and also the Maharani of Jaipur, obtaining her palace for a 'Pink Ball', reflecting the colours of the houses of the two cities. A week-long extravaganza ensued in March 2014, with reelers arriving at the venues in gaily decorated tuk-tuks; being showered with rose petals; entertained by fire-eaters, snake charmers, Bollywood dancers; flying kites and even playing polo on elephants.

Above: A graceful couple dancing in front of the Royal Opera House, Muscat

Photo courtesy of Dena Woodhams

Left: Omani horsemen entertaining guests before a desert ceilidh

Photo courtesy of Dena Woodhams

Mustering in the garden of the Al Bustan Palace Hotel, Muscat, Oman
Photo courtesy of Dena Woodhams

Dena is exceptional at networking. Back in Italy again, this time for an assembly in Florence in 2016, she gathered the support of the mayor, church dignitaries and the grand Florentine families who opened the doors of the Palazzo Corsini for a pre-ball practice and the Palazzo Vecchio for the main dance. There was also a memorable service in the Duomo, where there are carvings of angels playing bagpipes. Eight Scottish pipers topped and tailed the service with their final strains echoing round the cathedral for 12 haunting seconds.

The swansong was Oman in 2018 – the final 'Scots Abroad' reeling ball and one where I was lucky enough to be a guest. Mark and Dena again had a stalwart sponsor, Bruno Schroder, who paid for the band and they otherwise

A painting of all the 'Scots Abroad' balls
Artist: Bex Stanley

set about persuading the Omani powers-that-be to agree to venues, timing and local entertainment. That included a cruise in a dhow and a wonderful Desert Ceilidh by a Muscat beach where hundreds of Bedouins raced along the sand on camels and horsemen stood astride two galloping steeds, a foot on each one! We dined at tables named after the creatures of Oman – Saluki, Ibis, Falcon, Oryx – then danced 'Speed the Plough' and the other main reels late into the night.

Dena's attention to detail is legendary. As in Oman she ensured the tables in Italy, for instance, were named in keeping with the place: therefore, Italian artists like Bernini or types of pasta like tortellini. She speaks six languages fluently, was born in Kansas, brought up in Brazil, learnt Scottish dancing in her teens, moved to London in her twenties and attended the Perth Ball which bolstered her passion for everything Scottish. 'I love what happens to people when they reel,' she elaborates. 'Because I come from a dysfunctional family and was very nomadic, building bridges was always important to me. With Scottish dancing all bridges fall away and everyone becomes one cohesive unit.'

A glowing example of just that was the Indian guides joining the reels alongside the Maharajah of Jodhpur, who in turn was dancing 'The Dashing White Sergeant' with a little Italian girl who declared she felt like a princess in a fairy-tale.

A couple who travelled to two of the international balls – India in 2014 and Florence in 2016 – are Christopher and Rosamund Wynterbee-Robey. They praised the way both events were organised 'with military efficiency without being military'. They cite the Skye Ball, by contrast, as quite strict, having a Grand Vizier type at the entrance who turns away any lady whose dress is not floor length and a ban on 'helicopters' in the crowded hall. Christopher and Rosamund also went to the Waterloo Ball in Belgium in 2015 and joined the throng of 1,100 reelers at the Palace of Versailles in May 2022, making new friends and meeting up with old ones at all those balls.

Another pair who relish reeling balls are Jamie MacDonald and his wife Julia (née Hailes, MBE). Their favourite dance,

Jamie MacDonald and his wife, Julia Hailes, lifelong and enthusiastic reelers

always on the programme, is 'Mairi's Wedding' which they had at their wedding on the banks of Loch Fyne. Julia states that Jamie despaired of her style 'initially as I got in a muddle and now because I get carried away, raising my arms (tut-tutted) and banging bottoms in 'The Reel of the 51st Division'. Well, I lean my backside toward his and he shies away which onlookers find hilarious.' Happily, anyway, partners change partners, cliques split up and everyone dances with everyone else. 'It's a big ice-breaker,' Julia continues. 'We went on holiday in Kenya and taught our Samburu guides 'The Eightsome'. We were all beaming and laughing. Reeling is borderless.'

Samburu tribesmen learning 'The Reel of Three' for 'The Eightsome Reel'
Photo: Julia Hailes

The pinnacle of all the balls the MacDonalds have been to was India 2014. Julia recalls 'reeling under the night sky, whirling dervishes, fireworks… only Dena could have pulled it off… nobody else could have conceived of something so bonkers!' I wondered how Julia had fared on top of an elephant playing polo: 'I'm so competitive I desperately wanted to win. I managed, at least, to hit the ball before another elephant stood on it.' Since 2014 when the Indian ball took place, some countries have banned elephant polo. Its erstwhile supporters would argue that the slow-paced game is much less arduous for elephants than their former task of hauling logs. Anyhow, at the tournament cited, the elephants ruled. When they lost interest in the match it was promptly abandoned.

Balls of a different kind – and elephants in pursuit of them. A game of elephant polo before a dance in India in 2014
Photo courtesy of Dena Woodhams

Amongst the guests in India were some from New York where Jamie used to work. In 1978 he and some other expatriate Scots living in New York organised a party to teach reels to their American friends. The society continues to this day. Meanwhile, Jamie often runs dance classes and ceilidhs in Dorset (where he is based) and other parts of southern England. Without being imposing he manages to get scores of people, including novices, onto the floor, going more or less in the right direction and enjoying themselves. He admits, 'It's very rewarding knowing I'm responsible for that.' Like his brother-in-law Andy Campbell (of *The Swinging Sporran*), he applauds well-mannered men who steady their partners after spinning and women who offer some resistance, not being floppy as they swing.

The New York reelers – the group Jamie MacDonald helped establish – has one big ball every year. This takes place on a Saturday in November, preceded by some reeling practices led by Christopher Gow. The venue recently has been the Down Town Association (a handsome private club in Manhattan) with live music from the Iona Dance Band which also plays at the group's summer ceilidh. The committee of seven, headed by Alessandra Gagliardi, has collaborated with other relevant groups – piping associations, waltz and ballroom societies, the Caledonia Club of New York, the National Trust for Scotland and the University of St Andrews NYC Alumni Club – in order to boost numbers, which sank to zero during the pandemic. Now attendance is up to around 75 guests, many of whom have a common interest in Scotland either through ancestry or friends. Couples and individuals with or without partners are all welcome. The New York ball covers the main reels and the prized 'Reel of the 51st Division' is danced at least twice.

In Canada – where most early emigrants from Scotland settled – there are huge balls, probably the largest in the world. Montreal's Victory Ball in 1945 had 2,200 guests, including 171 debutantes, and it still attracts hundreds of dancers, though only a handful of 'debs' nowadays. The Toronto St Andrew's Charity Ball caters for up to a thousand guests at the Fairmont Royal York Hotel where, apart from function rooms for the elegant dinner, there is a ballroom measuring 12,843 square feet (1,193 metres). The Toronto Ball has been going for almost a hundred years whilst the charity it supports, the St Andrew's Charitable Foundation, was set up

Debutantes in white dresses and their escorts dancing at the Montreal Ball

International Photo Imaging

The Fairmont Royal York Hotel – venue for the Toronto St Andrew's Charity Ball

Photo: Michele Dalgarno

Dancers at a Toronto Ball
Photo: Michele Dalgarno

'Highlandin6' team of Highland Dancers poised to entertain the guests at the Toronto Ball
Photo: Michele Dalgarno

in 1836, originally to help Scottish immigrants who had fallen on hard times. Profits from the ball, both from sponsors and ticket sales (at $250 for dinner and dancing, $80 for dancing after 9.00pm), have topped $1 million (Canadian) over the past 15 years and now go to a range of local concerns. The programme has a mix of reels, SCD and ceilidh favourites – about 18 in all including repeats of the most popular ones ('Strip the Willow' and 'Waltz Country Dance'). Adding to the spectacle are the pipers in scarlet kilts and lively displays from the 'Highlandin6 Dancers'.

Down under there are nine SCD branches in Australia and about 90 clubs spread across eight regions in New Zealand. Several of those organise special parties, notably in 2023, the centenary of the Royal Scottish Country Dance Society. For instance, dancers from the Wellington, Rangitikei, Hawkes Bay and other regions gathered for a ball in Palmerston North on 4th November 2023. The Balmoral Band played the music for the 19 dances, which included 'Miss Milligan's Strathspey' and 'Mrs Stewart's Jig' (as a homage to the RSCDS founders) and 14 dances devised by New Zealanders. Amongst those were Ken Shaw's 'Morison's Bush', Romaine Butterfield's 'Catch the Wind' and Barry Skelton's 'Pelorus Jack', the last being inspired by a dolphin that was famous for meeting and escorting ships through a stretch of water near Cook Strait between 1888 and 1912. The guests at the Palmerston North ball included NZ Branch president Linda Glavin, and the Wellington Region president, Rod Downey, presented a tribute to Edith Campbell for having taught and organised SCD in Wellington for 60-odd years.

Grand March at the RSCDS centenary ball held in Palmerston North, New Zealand, in November 2023

Photo: Loralee Hyde

Dancing 'Morison's Bush' at the RSCDS centenary ball

Photo: Loralee Hyde

Rod Downey, Wellington region president of the RSCDS, presenting a tribute to Edith Campbell for her sterling work for the branch

Photo: Loralee Hyde

Whilst SCD (and the occasional ceilidh) are well known in the Antipodes, reeling is virtually unheard of. Even so, in New Zealand in February 2020 there was a terrific reeling ball to rival the ones spearheaded by Mark Tennant and Dena Woodhams. In fact, it was Dena who encouraged Wellington resident Lady Lilias Bell to organise it. Called the 'Southern Meeting', it attracted many of the reelers who had patronised the 'Scots Abroad' balls with 80 people flying in from the UK, USA, Canada, Denmark, Portugal, Singapore and Australia. Along with local Caledonian enthusiasts there

Lady Lilias and Johnny Bell in Dunedin, New Zealand, on the steps of Larnach Castle, the venue for the Southern Meeting ball held in February 2020
Photo: Nicola Wilkins

The Schiehallion Band outside Larnach Castle (whose ballroom was modelled on the one at Blair Castle in Scotland), before playing for the reelers at the ball
Photo: Nicola Wilkins

were eventually 114 guests all gathered by Lady Bell.

She is the sister of Donald Graham and sister-in-law of Bridie, my hosts at the Northern Meeting in 2023. As well as her impeccable Scottish credentials, she is married to a Kiwi and reels superbly. Lilias was keen to ensure that guests coming from afar would be dancing with others who knew how to reel. Accordingly, she spent several weekends in 2019 going to other cities to run practices of the ten classic reels. She also realised that if people were travelling all the way to New Zealand they would want more than a single ball. So, she booked Martinborough Town Hall for an informal Picnic Ball which, unlike its Northern Meeting counterpart 11,300 miles north, preceded the main event, the grand ball held at Larnach Castle in Dunedin. That city was the perfect choice because of its Scottish roots – Dunedin was designed in the 1800s as a 'new Edinburgh' – whilst Larnach Castle has a

Gorgeous reeling at Larnach Castle
Nicola Wilkins

fine ballroom created as a replica of the one at Blair Atholl.

There were some challenges as Lilias recalls: 'There was an audible gasp from the band when I asked them to play from 10.00pm to 2.00am. Scottish Country Dances in New Zealand start and end much earlier.' Then the dreaded Covid emerged. Several people, including some crucial single men, had booked to fly through China and they were grounded. However, Lilias was able to enlist some male dancers from the Royal New Zealand Ballet to make up the sets. Neither she nor the guests had foreseen the widespread and deadly nature of the ensuing pandemic.

Against the odds, the Southern Meeting was a triumph and just in time before the country went into lockdown. The weather was perfect as the throng gathered for cocktails on the lawn in front of the castle. After dinner the Schiehallion Band had the reelers stamping, clapping, twirling and birling. Fittingly enough it was also called 'The Reel Thing' – and nobody assumed it was about fishing!

CHAPTER SIX

Ceilidhs

A CEILIDH – PRONOUNCED kay-lee – is basically a party. The word derives from Old Irish words meaning 'companion', 'visit', 'visiting' and the Scottish Gaelic word for 'gathering' – one which invariably includes music, dancing, food and drink. At more traditional ceilidhs there would also be storytelling, poetry and singing.

The dances are always simple and the venue dictates which ones are chosen. I went to a marvellous ceilidh in a family house on the banks of a loch in South Uist, the Outer Hebrides. The owners like dancing so have incorporated a large open plan living room with a wooden floor. In the middle, however, is a stylish, raised peat fire so we mainly danced around it in pairs doing, for instance, the 'Gay Gordons' and a jolly 'Highland Schottische'.

We squeezed in some sets for 'Strip the Willow' and 'The Reel of the 51st Division' with interludes to eat the food everybody had brought along; to take photos of the shaggy Highland cattle with heathery hills and a blazing sunset beyond them; and to listen to Western Islanders Ruraigh Gray and Annie MacDonald singing Gaelic airs (beautifully, each having won gold medals at the Mòd, a Gaelic cultural festival).

On the other side of the world, in the Falkland Islands,

Lochside Highland Cattle
Photo courtesy of Coorie Retreats

similar dances feature at the annual May ball in the capital, Stanley. An enterprising couple, Lee and Lisa Martin, teach teenagers waltzes and simple ceilidh dances (the only trickier one being 'The Dashing White Sergeant'). The Martins' classes on Wednesday evenings lead up to the hotly anticipated spring gathering. In advance the youths buy formal evening wear from online websites and turn out looking their best for the big do, much to the delight of adult relatives also attending.

John Carver (of London Reels) is another who runs ceilidhs for teenagers – for instance, at birthday parties, where he succeeds in getting youths to stop texting and start dancing. He is most in demand, though, at weddings where

John Carver 'calling' the dances
London Reels

ceilidhs are increasingly popular as entertainment after the ceremony. John nearly always suggests the Orcadian version of 'Strip the Willow' where the newly-weds start off turning each other and all the guests on both sides of a long set so that the bride and groom will have danced with everyone. To mix people up, he also favours the progressive 'Gay Gordons' where you have a new partner at each refrain. Other dances, not originally from Scotland but often scheduled at Scottish-style ceilidhs, include 'The Virginia Reel' and 'Circassian Circle' as people can get into the swing of them easily. John has introduced all those dances in all sorts of places: inside church halls or outside them on the grass, in old wooden barns and brand-new school gyms…

Wedding Ceilidh in a barn, organised by 'Licence to Ceilidh'
Lizzie Adams, Shoot it Momma (Rees Images)

In Edinburgh another man who 'calls' the dances at ceilidhs is David Francis. He has even written a Master's thesis on 'The Dance Caller in Scotland: Practice, Role and Function'. Whilst someone in charge at a ball would generally be called an MC, at the more informal ceilidh it is a 'caller'. Their role is to devise the programme of dances, persuade people on to the floor and provide directions, both in advance of the announced dance and during it. The caller would also, like an MC, announce, 'Now it's time for the raffle,' or 'We'll have a 10-minute break'.

David Francis, caller at ceilidhs and member of the Bella McNab dance band
Photo: Simon Baker

In keeping with the relaxed nature of ceilidhs, David Francis teaches the dances without appearing to do so. He has walk-throughs of each dance and explains everything clearly but without being bossy. He then picks up his guitar and joins his fellow musicians (the Bella McNab dance band), giving further instructions only if needed. 'People are quite good-natured,' he muses, 'If they're getting it wrong they generally dissolve into laughter.'

It is tricky manoeuvres that invariably go awry: walking

backwards in 'The Gay Gordons', facing 'corners' in 'The Duke of Perth'. So, David would keep the former until later in the evening and avoid the latter along with most of the traditional Scottish Country Dances. He has, however, trawled through all the RSCDS booklets in order to pick out dances suitable for ceilidhs. With those amongst his repertoire he has about 70 dances in his head or on cards. He can easily draw on one that is energetic (eg 'Strip the Willow') followed by something more leisurely like the 'Cumberland Reel' or 'Flowers of Edinburgh' where the top couple dances while others have a breather. He also might vary the standard programme with something unusual (but easy) – for instance, 'Hullichan's Jig'. His favourite ceilidh dance is 'The Waves of Tory' where couples swoop around or under arches.

There is no course or training manual for would-be callers. But David embodies the necessary qualities. His day job is at the Traditional Music Forum (which he directs) and being a musician, he is right on the beat. Thus, he can deliver an instruction – say, 'Get your right hands ready for the Grand Chain' – exactly when it is needed, a few beats before the actual manoeuvre. He knows all the dances and is able to project. 'You can't rely on a microphone,' he explains, 'If you mumble into a mic all you get is louder mumbling.'

He has professional engagements about once a month, calling for Parent Teacher Associations (adults and children), at public fundraising events, weddings and civil partnerships. 'At those,' David says, 'we tried to be politically correct, saying if you're on this side of the set we'll call you "dogs" and on the other "cats".' But he has now given up on the animal nomenclature, reverting to 'men' on one side, 'women' on the other. 'I don't care about your chromosomes,' he declares at gay ceilidhs, 'If you can put up with this temporary assignation it will be a lot easier for me.'

David used to worry about getting people's attention, particularly at weddings where all the guests are talking and drinking. 'Now it doesn't bother me. I might get just eight people up and onto the dance floor. Others can watch if they want and it contributes to the general atmosphere.' At public events where people have specifically come to dance it is a very different scene. Between 8.00 and 11.30pm people flock to the floor for the 18 or so dances that David would call – starting, usually, with the progressive 'Circassian Circle'. The best ceilidh he ever master-minded was a recent one at

Children at a ceilidh in Daliburgh, South Uist, in July 2024
Ceòlas

the Edinburgh International Harp Festival. 'Everyone was up and dancing, keen and able. Then there were interludes with people playing the harp – lovely!'

I wondered if he could immediately spot those who had reeled before or done SCD. 'Yes,' was the response. 'The Scottish Country Dancers turn up with their pumps and ghillies and are neater. The reelers have stiffer legs when setting, sway from the hips up and clap.' The story goes that Prince Charles, as he then was, engaged an RSCDS tutor to come to Balmoral to teach his boys, William and Harry, how to dance. But it was reeling that Charles was after so that tutor was soon sent away.

The style of dancing at ceilidhs is of minimal importance. But events are obviously more enjoyable if people know where they are going and it is the caller who puts them on the right track. 'The appeal of ceilidhs,' says David, 'is the sense you get of moving in concert with other people. You are dancing as an individual and with a partner within a set, which is one of several sets. It's a common endeavour, collective, congenial.' It is especially rewarding for the caller. As David explains, 'I have the task of turning this seething mass of people into a coherent whole. I like being the alchemist who makes the evening happen.'

CHAPTER SEVEN

Highland Dancing

AT THE OTHER end of the spectrum from ceilidhs is Highland Dancing. Whilst ceilidh dances are easy and sociable, the Highland Dances are complicated and are performed for applause or trophies. Groups of Highland Dancers, usually girls, often do displays – for example, at the charity ball in Toronto and at parties or concerts in Scotland – where proud relatives and admiring onlookers clap like mad. Alternatively, they are competing against each other at Highland Games, each contestant hoping to win a medal or cup.

Highland Dancers in New Zealand where all contestants wear Balmoral hats. Left to right: Evelyn Levett, Danielle Pope, Tannah Adam (née McLay), Megan Clark

Photo: Shiobhan Smith

Sword dancers being careful not to touch a blade
iStock

They are judged on four dances: the two most ancient ones, the Sword Dance and Highland Fling (which used to test and enhance the skills of warriors) as well as the Strathspey & Reel and 'Seann Triubhas'. This last dance, which means 'Old Trousers', dates from the 18th century when the Act of Prohibition banned kilts. Some people believe the leg kicks in 'Seann Triubhas' represent attempts to shake off the despicable trews. Certainly, kilts look better than trews and are the preferred attire of both male and female Highland Dancers, as the tartan material flicks up and flares out when the dancers leap or turn. All of them look immaculate, their hose (knee length socks) matching the tartan of their kilts, the women wearing velvet jackets edged

Highland dancer Lewis Gibson at a 2017 competition in New Zealand
Photo: Glenn Potter

in a bird wing shape (in white) at the back, the men sporting doublets and Balmoral hats.

The most prestigious competition worldwide is the Cowal Gathering held in Dunoon, west of Glasgow in Scotland. The three-day annual event has been going strong since it started in 1894 and it now attracts around 3,500 competitors: pipers, drummers, 'heavies' (tossing the caber or wrestling) and Highland dancers. The dancing is organised by the Royal Scottish Official Board of Highland Dancing (RSOBHD). There are trophies for Highland Dancers from Argyll aged four and over, but the most prized silver cups are for the World Championships, divided into three categories: Juveniles (aged 12 to 15), Juniors (aged 16 to 17) and Adults (18+). At the 2023 games I attended, over 600 of the dance competitors had come from as far away as Canada, USA, South Africa and Australia.

To process the hundreds of dancers who have managed to qualify for Cowal, the contest is carefully arranged with heats leading to the finals. At one round, for example, the Juniors wait their turn to the left of a raised platform while the Adults queue up on the right. Eight dancers then line up downstage, four Juniors on the left, four Adults on the right, with a piper ready to play behind them. Three judges are seated below the stage on the Junior side, three more on the other side to appraise the Adults. The dancers, each with a number attached to their kilt, stand erect with their feet turned out (in 'First Position'), bow to the judges, await the Piper's first skirmishes then on the beat start the first of the four dances. If, woe betide, one of the dancers makes a mistake, like touching a blade in the Sword Dance, he or she quietly bows to the judges and withdraws. After those eight dancers have completed a dance, the next eight take their turn. The running order for the dancers varies, but the dances themselves go in strict sequence: Highland Fling, Sword Dance, Seann Triubhas, Reel. There is a new crop of judges for each of the four dances.

What, I wondered, are the judges looking for in choosing the 20 (in each section) to go into the finals and then the winning dancer in each age group? To enlighten me I talked to Billy Forsyth, twice winner of the World Highland Dance Championships who has adjudicated at dance competitions on every continent. 'Elevation and turn out play a part,' he explained, 'but it's primarily technique – neat footwork and being right on the beat.' His views are endorsed by Christine Lacey, herself a former champion, and chair of the RSOBHD, who hands out the cups to the winning dancers. Christine's sister-in-law, Diane Macphee Krugh, from Houston, Texas, also used to do Highland Dancing, then taught it and has been coming to Cowal for 40 years. She told me that, 'To be really good at Highland Dancing you need the strength of a gymnast and the grace of a ballerina.' Certainly the best of the contestants, including Michelle Gordon and Candice Walker the day I was there, demonstrated those qualities, leaping high into the air and landing quietly time and again.

To add to the challenge, the four competition dances differ slightly from year to year. Billy Forsyth explained that there are, for instance, three or four different ways to do the 'crossover' step in 'The Highland Fling'. The championship

'The Sailor's Hornpipe' performed by Imogen Grayson from New Zealand
Photo: Glenn Potter

Rugby player Jorja Miller, who attributes her speed and agility to years of training as a Highland Dancer
Photosport NZ. Photo: Iain McGregor

board in, say, 2025, nominate one of those methods for the following year so the dancers learn a new routine for 2026. Outside of the competitions there are other dances – for instance, 'The Sailor's Hornpipe'. That was the favourite of a New Zealand former Highland Dance national champion, Jorja Miller, who now plays rugby for her country (which won the Rugby 7s Gold at the Paris Olympics). Jorja attributes her bounce, agility and fleetness of foot to years of training as a dancer. More Highland Dances include 'Flora MacDonald's Fancy', 'Scottish Lilt', 'Barracks Johnnie' and 'Highland Laddie'.

Probably the most famous Highland lad in the dancing world is Gareth Mitchelson from Monifieth. He started, at the age of six, learning Highland Dance from his mother, Wilma Tomie, herself a world champion. After competing at Braemar ('always freezing cold') and several other Scottish games, Gareth went on to win the adult Highland Dance championship at Cowal four times, the first being in 1985 when his brother, Deryck, won the Juvenile section. Gareth reckons the Highland Fling is the hardest dance, having 50 steps which are harder still to execute if the music speeds up. 'My mum danced it at 160 beats a minute but the tempo nowadays is down to 112 beats a minute. I once raced through it at 192 beats to the minute!' I asked him why so few men are Highland Dancing today. Originally there were just men competing at the Highland games, but their numbers went down during and after the two world wars. 'So,' says Gareth, 'the girls came in. I wish more men would do it now, but I haven't the answer as to how. It's egalitarian, men and women competing against each other. The best dancer wins.'

To date, the dancer deemed 'the best' having won more trophies than anyone else is Colleen Rintamaki. In fact, she is the most decorated Highland Dance World Champion ever, winning the Juvenile section twice (first in 1995), the Juniors twice and the Adults six times (finally in 2005). This ten times world champion also won the Canadian Championships 14 times. Colleen, from Ontario, was doing tap and ballet aged four. She went to a birthday party and saw another little girl dancing 'The Sailor's Hornpipe'. Inspired by that, she set about learning it and other Highland Dances being much

Ten times world champion Highland Dancer, Colleen Rintamaki, with one of her many trophies struck by older Canadians preeminent in the field: Carleigh Leighton, for instance, joyful in her Royal Blue kilt, and Estelle Clewes with her high cuts looking as though she were flying.

Colleen's own ascent involved decades of training with her teacher, Joy Tolev, and a lot of sacrifice: no partying with her high school friends on Friday nights (because of competitions on Saturday); less space for her whole family as her parents converted first their basement and then the garage into a dance studio for Colleen. Despite all the effort – and expense of tuition, travel and flights – top marks were not a given. In 1994, for example, when downpours at Cowal meant everyone had to crowd into the Queen's Hall, Colleen (then aged 13) was upset by the heats being delayed and having to dance on the side near the judges – and she came third. However, the setback caused her to change her attitude, turning negatives into positives, and with that state of mind she was on to her winning streak.

By 1995 Colleen's past triumphs and assured future prompted the BBC to send a film crew to Cowal to cover her every move for a documentary, *That Fling Thing*. That, in turn, raised her public profile and there were many rewards. She dined with Queen Elizabeth II, performed for the former Canadian Prime Minister, Jean Chretien, danced with other world champions including who she describes as 'the Mitchelson boys', and did a workshop tour in New Zealand where she was impressed by champion in the making, Morgan Bamford, and by the different styles of Highland Dancing there.

The Piping and Dancing Association is the governing body for most of New Zealand's Highland and National Dancing

Morgan Bamford doing 'The Leap' at end of 'Seann Triubhas'
Photo: *Taranaki Daily News*

competitions, with technique set by the New Zealand Academy of Highland and National Dancing. Neither organisation is affiliated with the RSOBHD and Highland Dancing in New Zealand differs from what is deemed the 'official' style elsewhere. For instance, a Scottish or Canadian dancer would have the pointed foot vertical with the supporting leg for the first round of the leg movements of the Highland Fling whilst a New Zealander would stretch the point foot fully. All Highland Dancing girls have their hair tied back or up but New Zealand girls also wear Balmoral hats.

Colleen has now moved on from all the gear and exertions of Highland Dancing, being a mother and a Director of Sales.

Another Canadian champion, Marielle Lesperance, with her baby
Photo courtesy of Will McLernon and Rob Short

But she recognises how helpful her dancing career has been. 'Because of it,' she elaborates, 'I'm good at setting goals and reaching them. I take on board both criticism and feedback, and from them work out how to improve. I know how to mask nerves and address audiences – though I do still tend to start with my feet turned out in first position. I had a boss who said, "You're standing like a duck!"'

Another remarkable dancer, again from Canada, is Marielle Lespérance. She won her eighth world title at Cowal in 2022 having had a three-year break and a baby. There is some internet footage of her adorable infant, Margaux, crawling

World champions 2022: from left, Annalise Lam (Junior), Marielle Lesperance (Adult), Lily Kelman (Juvenile)
Photo: Ronnie Cairns

around on the floor while Marielle tries to practise her steps. The disrupted schedule was a considerable challenge, but Marielle had seen other new mothers succeed in recent Olympics. With that impetus she persevered and, accompanied by her husband and baby Margaux, she arrived at Cowal. There, she outranked the other 90 adult contestants, winning all four dances with 11 out of the 12 judges putting her at the top of their score cards. She was 33 and the first mother in Cowal's long history to win the championship. Deryck Mitchelson, convening, said, 'She is a unique talent. We've never seen anybody that's been able to continue to the same sort of age as Marielle and be so dominant.' Most dancers hit their peak in their early- to mid-20s. 'She's unflappable,' Mitchelson continued, 'She's graceful, she's got precision and she finishes her dances as strongly as she starts them which is quite unusual. She makes it look so easy.'

In 2025 Marielle returned to Cowal and triumphed becoming the Adult World Champion again. Besides competing she now runs her own dance school in Dartmouth, Nova Scotia. She choreographs a fusion of Highland Dance with modern influences for public performances with her highland dance company, Change of Step.

The success of champions Marielle Lespérance, Colleen Rintamaki, the Mitchelson brothers and Bobby Forsyth – both as Highland Dancers and in their subsequent careers – help motivate the next aspiring dancers. One such is Lily Kelman from Inverness, who already has a title under her belt, having won the World Juvenile Championship (the

Lily Kelman (second right) with her family in Dunoon, 2023

Lily Kelman from Inverness competing at Cowal in 2023
Photo: John Stewart

youngest category) in 2022. She started when she was a mere two-year-old following in the footsteps of her mother, Yvonne, and grandmother, Irene, who were both Highland Dancers. Those two and teacher Fiona MacNeil are Lily's greatest supporters, but she also has a sister, Grace, who plays the pipes and sometimes accompanies her as well as a musical father, Jason, who helps keep the show on the road.

I met all of them at Cowal, at Hunter's Quay holiday village, before the qualifying heats. A family friend, a boy dancer, was just leaving, which got us going on the difference between male

Canadian siblings Macgregor and Aisla Gocan-Wright, with their Highland Dancing trophies

Photo: Alissia Gocan-Wright

Macgregor Gocan-Wright in mid 'Highland Fling' at Cowal in 2023
Photo: Clare Marie-Bailie

The Gocan-Wrights taking trophies in their stride
Photo: Alissia Gocan-Wright

and female dancers. According to Lily the boys normally have more strength and power than the girls, but girls can surpass them in elevation, technique, turn-out and presence. 'So who,' I asked, 'are your main opponents?' 'Everybody!' she exclaimed. Sadly, a torn calf muscle scuppered her chances at the last Cowal gathering. But with her competitive spirit, great charm and undoubted abilities, Lily Kelman will be back.

Another World Champion is Aisla Gocan-Wright who, like Lily before her, won the Juvenile section at Cowal in 2024, aged 13, winning it again, a year later, in 2025. Her favourite dance is an interactive one, the Full Hullachan (or 'Full Reel of Tulloch') which incorporates elements from all the Highland dances. Aisla, from Ontario, practices for up to two hours every day and enjoys the muscle burn after each session as well as the adrenaline rush and excitement of competing. Following hard on her heels is her younger brother, Macgregor, who has also won trophies and relishes the challenge of Highland Dancing, both mental and physical. Like fellow Canadian Colleen Rintamaki (and Jorja Miller from New Zealand), Macgregor is smitten with the Hornpipe – 'I like how I get to portray a sailor and how intricate the footwork is.' Both children appreciate the input of their mother, Alissia, a teacher of Highland Dancing, whose support motivates them to strive and improve. 'My ultimate goal,' says Macgregor, 'is to be as talented and hard-working as my sister and hopefully be a World Champion too.' Watch this space!

CHAPTER EIGHT

Step Dance

ONE GENRE OF Scottish dancing that is little known in Scotland itself is Step Dance. This is not to be confused with the more balletic 'Ladies Step' which had to change its name (to 'Scottish Step') to be more gender neutral – despite the fact it is very much geared for women in soft pumps. Hard-shoe Step Dance used to be common in Scotland, but it then left Scottish shores along with the many Scots who emigrated in the 18th and 19th centuries. However, the emigrants kept their Scottish culture and those who landed in North-East Canada carried on Step Dancing.

It was and remains especially popular in Cape Breton, in Nova Scotia, and it was Cape Breton Step Dancers, including Harvey Beaton and Mary Janet Macdonald, who brought this type of dancing back to Scotland in the 1990s. Three decades later it is gaining momentum, with Step Dance courses arranged annually on the islands of Skye and South Uist, the Scottish Stepdance Company performing at festivals and individuals like Sophie Stephenson running Step Dance workshops throughout the UK (and Europe). Credit is due to a Swedish man, Mats Melin, who has spent years researching and reviving Step Dance (as well as Hebridean Dance and quadrilles).

Step Dance is a form of percussive dance, like clog or tap

Step dancer Harvey MacKinnon, a legend in his native Nova Scotia
Photo courtesy of Harvey MacKinnon

Step dancer Sophie Stephenson in the Scottish Highlands
Photo courtesy of Sophie Stephenson

dancing but lighter on the feet. By beating one's heels and toes in hard-soled shoes, the dancer becomes the drums to the accompanying piper, fiddler or singer. The closest parallel would be Irish 'Sean-Nós', which has similarly fast and precise movements of the feet. But Scottish Step Dance differs from its Irish counterpart in being more relaxed and fluid, without the stiff upper body of Irish dancing (made famous by 'Riverdance').

Sophie Stephenson is from the Scottish Highlands and she started learning ballet, tap and Highland Dancing from the age of two. Later in her childhood she was introduced to Step Dance through classes at local Gaelic festivals. She was particularly inspired by a performance at a church hall in Inverness with Harvey Beaton step dancing and Buddy McMaster playing the fiddle. 'I was itching to join them,' Sophie told me. 'I love how the dance fits the music, is so laid back yet intricate and driven.' She went on to attend a Step Dance course on Skye where her innate ability propelled her, aged 11, into the advanced class with adults. Perhaps it runs in the blood. A forebear of hers, Alasdair Gillies, a dance master in Scotland, emigrated in 1826 to Cape Breton where he carried on teaching Step Dance! Two centuries later, Sophie, his great-great-great-great niece, has also travelled to Canada to meet dancers and learn new steps as practised in Quebec, Ottawa, Nova Scotia and 'Acadian' style in Newfoundland. She is delighted that Step Dance has been reintroduced to Scotland where she now teaches it to small groups, whenever she is not performing or running workshops at big festivals like Celtic Connections in Glasgow or the Festival Interceltique de Lorient in Brittany.

In July 2024 I learnt some Step Dancing from a Cape Breton tutor, Tara Rankin, running the intermediate course at Ceòlas, based at Daliburgh on South Uist. In a church hall with a wooden floor, Tara taught us Tippy Tappy (step, kick, hop, back) and other Strathspeys (Circle, Triangle, Travelling Side Step); as well as Reels (Basic, Doubled-up Shuffle, Stamp Shuffle, Harvey Beaton) and two jigs (Basic and Doubled-up). Meanwhile the advanced class, taught by another Cape Bretoner, Gerard Beaton, were doing the same steps (faster) and others which were more complicated.

All my fellow students had already been to Step Dance

Ceòlas, the base for Gaelic and Step Dance courses in Daliburgh, with the South Uist flag in the foreground

Ceòlas

Gerard Beaton from Cape Breton, leading a Step Dance class at Ceòlas

Ceòlas

Morag and Neil MacPherson, teachers of ceilidh dances and quadrilles

classes, in Glasgow for instance, and at previous courses at Ceòlas – a combination of the Gaelic words 'Ceòl' (music) and 'Eòlas' (knowledge). Ceòlas, running since 1996, is a week-long celebration, with tuition, of the Gaelic language and songs, harp and fiddle playing, piping, Step Dance and quadrilles. The latter are taught by Neil and Morag

MacPherson, whose class I attended at Ceòlas as an optional extra. The couple run sessions throughout the year in the Hebrides, teaching ceilidh dances and the lively quadrilles which combine SCD and Barn Dance formations. Generally, Morag instructs and Neil demonstrates, partnered by a nimble friend of theirs, Mary Godden. Apart from the Step Dance and quadrille classes at Ceòlas, there are concerts, lectures, music in pubs and time in between for walks around beautiful Eriskay or swims in clear, sandy coves. Altogether it makes for a brilliant holiday. For years Helen Deeney, in my intermediate Step Dance class, has been coming to Ceòlas, its initial letter reminding her of other 'C's that win her approval: 'the company, cakes, ceilidhs and craic – they're all great!'

As for Step Dancing, Helen likes 'the freedom of it and the sound of the feet'. Also in my class was Isobel Kyle who appreciates being able to get up and dance without needing a partner and having the chance to be creative, assembling steps in whichever way one chooses. Another Ceòlas intermediate, Fiona Halliday, from New Zealand but now living in Scotland, likes how friendly and non-competitive Step Dancing is. Fiona has been to Cape Breton where she saw tiny children, hardly walking, already Step Dancing. 'It's a community thing,' Fiona says, 'It's just what you do there: men and women, young and old.'

Our Canadian tutor, Tara Rankin, told us how her grandfather, an expert Step Dancer, had had 15 children. All of his descendants Step Dance, Tara starting at the comparatively old age of seven. Traditionally Cape Breton

Fellow step dance student, Fiona Halliday, above a loch before a dance on South Uist

houses were small, but Step Dance could be done in minimal space hence the appeal of a 'kitchen dance' executed on a hard floor and on the spot. It is not thereby a solitary dance, since it is usually done in bars or at parties with people watching. Moreover, Step Dancers can gather for a Scotch Four and at ceilidhs there are square dances.

The form is as follows: the ceilidh starts at 9.00pm with everyone joining in a communal dance of the district. For instance, there is the 'Inverness County Set' where square sets of eight people do half a Grand Chain (where alternate dancers circle clockwise or anti-clockwise). They then swing partners, complete the Grand Chain, promenade. The top couple (nearest the band) then gallop down the middle of all the sets and back up the sides. Everyone joins hands in a large circle and Step Dances however they please. The sets reform, repeat and the bottom couple lead up and back. At midnight is the 'Dancer Cue' when individuals casually move into a central spot and do a minute or two of Step Dancing. I asked Tara what happened if some show-off carries on, hogging the floor. 'Hopefully another dancer would start,' she replied, 'or the fiddle player just stops!'

Although Tara now lives in Scotland she has fond memories of the Cape Breton ceilidhs: one at West Mabou Hall on Saturday night for infants to 90 year olds; another at Brook Village for those over 19 (being licensed premises); and famously at Glencoe Mills deep in the countryside. 'You drive for 20 minutes down a dirt road,' Tara explains. 'It's pitch black with trees on both sides and bears in the woods. You think you're lost. Then suddenly you see the lights of Glencoe Hall and hear music playing. It's wonderful!'

The hub for Step Dancing on a daily basis in Cape Breton is Mabou, where there is also a school running a week-long course in late July for aspiring Step Dancers. Tara was a Mabou student, her fellow countryman, Gerard Beaton, taught there and both pay tribute to the organiser, Melody Cameron, who they describe as 'a phenomenal dancer with great steps'. Other luminaries include Harvey MacKinnon, Willie Fraser, Margie Beaton (no relation) and Mac Morin – all of whom are light on their feet and bring their own personality and ideas into their Step Dancing. There are tales of people dancing on tea trays or the stumps of tree trunks.

Margie Beaton
Photo courtesy of Margie Beaton

The greatest compliment, according to Gerard, is to say that someone 'could dance on the head of a pin'. Certainly, Gerard himself has the tidy footwork he praises – judging by my observation of him teaching the advanced students at Ceòlas. But he also looks relaxed, loose-limbed – at least from the ankles up.

Amongst his Ceòlas class were Clara Camesse from Quimper in Brittany. She started Step Dancing ten years ago at Skye with Sophie Stevenson and then in Mabou with Melody Cameron. Clara is now a fine dancer, readily doing a solo turn after Gerard and Tara at one of the ceilidhs. Back in France, Clara often does a Step Dance demonstration at cafés or informal concerts with her partner, Yann Cariou, playing the pipes. Her compatriots are impressed. Their usual

Gerard Beaton at a Ceòlas ceilidh, with Tara Rankin on keyboard and Kyle MacDonald playing the fiddle
Ceòlas

reaction, she is proud to say, is 'Wow!'

Frank McConnell is another making an impact – both at Ceòlas refreshing his steps in the advanced class and as a key figure resurrecting Step Dance in Scotland. From the 1990s onwards he joined forces with Buddy McMaster and Harvey Beaton from Cape Breton; Mats Melin from Sweden; and fellow Scots Sandra Robertson, Maggie Moore, Mairi Campbell, Alison Carlisle, John Sikorski and Caroline Rae

Clara Camesse, a keen step dancer from Brittany

to showcase Step Dance where it had originated, in Scotland. Frank McConnell was one of several teaching the steps, in his case at a summer school in Benbecula, later joining the Dannsa troupe which performs to this day. Like all the best Step Dancers, Frank has rhythm inside him. Even a stroke a few years ago has not stopped him in his stride.

Step Dance now has a young cohort to keep it going in Scotland. Eibhlin Milne, for instance, a woman in her 20s, is a keen and regular attendant at the Ceòlas Step Dancing

Frank McConnell, a leading light in Step Dance and its revival in Scotland

course. She plans to start classes for children in her home city, Dundee. She has already had a trial run which worked well as she promises her young charges, 'You get to be the drums.' Eibhlin notes that, 'It's unusual and nice for kids, being allowed to be loud.' It is also inspiring for the boys seeing men dancing, even if it is just videos of Gerard Beaton and his fellow countrymen Step Dancing in Cape Breton.

CHAPTER NINE

Music and Musicians

AN INTEGRAL PART of all Scottish dancing is the music. The most common accompanying instrument is the accordion, but bagpipes, fiddles, keyboards and drums are often called into play – either as solo instruments or joining with others to make a double act, trio, quartet or band.

The tunes they play range from the earliest ones like 'Speed the Plough' (first documented in 1790) to more recent ones like 'Seton's Ceilidh Band', a dance devised by Bruce Fordyce who also wrote the music for it (in 1961). Amongst composers of Scottish dance melodies we should pay tribute to the great musicians of the 18th century: Mackintosh, Marshall, Fraser and the two Gows, Niel and his son Nathaniel. Niel Gow was patronised by three Dukes of Atholl, hence his portrait in their ancestral seat, Blair Castle. He composed over 80 tunes and was lauded by Burns for the way he played 'his wondrous fiddle' in his poem 'To Mr Gow, Visiting Dumfries'. Like the poet, Gow enjoyed more than a wee dram of whisky. Apparently, after one bibulous dance at Blair Castle he was zig zagging home and joined by a friend who commiserated with him on the distance Gow had to walk. 'It's not the length of the road that worries me,' Gow replied, 'It's the breadth!'

Many of the Scottish dance musicians have more than one

Niel Gow, portrait by Sir Henry Raeburn
From the collection at Blair Castle, Perthshire

string to their bow. 'Dancie' Reid, for example, born John Reid in 1869, could play his fiddle and dance simultaneously. There is some faded, wobbly footage of Dancie Reid playing his violin and teaching a dance at the St Andrews Summer

Luke Brady (front left) and his band
Photo courtesy of RSCDS

School in the years before he died (in 1942). He was also a judge at highland dance and piping competitions.

Luke Brady, the current Music Director of the RSCDS, is another who multi-tasks. He selects music for the dance books the society publishes; directs bands in studios recording tracks for dance CDs; has his own Luke Brady Scottish Dance Band which performs at numerous events; and plays the accordion (his main instrument) and the piano. He played the piano for the dance class I was in at St Andrews – with great skill as he has worked with ballet companies for years. Luke prioritises the needs of dancers. 'If the class is struggling with the rhythm,' he told me, 'you emphasise the beat while playing the melody. If the teacher wants the steps to be more precise, you pull back the music and make it lighter. If the dancers need to drive out their steps, you play with more gusto to make it clearer.' Luke recognises he is there to serve

Kyle MacDonald from Cape Breton, who plays the fiddle accompanying Step Dancers
Ceòlas

others – although he could easily earn applause playing flashy pieces like the notoriously difficult 'Lady Harriet Hope's Reel' (also the tune for 'Mrs Stewart of Fasnacloich'). One of his favourite tunes is a Strathspey, 'Minister on the Loch', composed by Muriel Johnstone as a tribute to Robert MacKay, another Summer School musician who was a very dapper gentleman, rather like 'The Skating Minister' of Sir Henry Raeburn's famous painting.

The most common instruments for Step Dance are the fiddle and keyboard. Three outstanding practitioners at Ceòlas 2024 were Kyle MacDonald on the violin and Kolten MacDonnell and Tara Rankin at the keyboard, all from Cape Breton. Kyle is very much a Canadian countryman – bearded, laid back, talking about the many 'toons' that 'folks' in Nova Scotia play, which may have been composed by them or recollected from their Scottish forbears. He approves of the stance of eminent Cape Breton musician John Donald Cameron, who advocated finding the oldest sheet music for a tune and regarding that as the skeleton, like a Christmas tree which you then decorate as you please. Certainly, Kyle is an inventive player and a vigorous one, broken strings flying from the top of his bow. Aged six he was told to, 'Get angry at the fiddle. Don't be dainty. Don't be rough or scratchy either but imitate the confidence of the pipes.'

For extra volume back in Cape Breton, to ensure the dancers could hear the music, fiddlers' wives used to add the click of their knitting needles. Now the norm is for the fiddler to start the tune and the pianist to join in, jamming. Their aim is to play with such verve some bystander will be impelled to get onto the floor. The musicians do not want what has been termed 'a dry set' where nobody responds to the dancer's cue.

For Step Dance classes where volume is of less concern there is sometimes 'Puirt-à-beul' (pronounced 'Purshtabeal'), which is a Gaelic term meaning 'tunes from the mouth'. At my Ceòlas class we were blessed in having Eilidh Cormack, a young woman from Skye, who is used to singing for dancing.

Eilidh Cormack from the Isle of Skye singing tunes to accompany Step Dancing at Ceòlas
Ceòlas

She and the teacher, Tara, would confer about the rhythm required for the next set of steps and Eilidh, sitting above us on the stage, would sing something in a Strathspey, Reel or Jig tempo. The words, she admitted, are nonsensical or mundane (about porridge, getting drunk at Christmas, a new set of shoes...) but the crucial thing is singing firmly and with a steady beat so the dancers can absorb the rhythm and transfer it to their feet.

Eilidh's boyfriend, Seonaidh MacIntyre, plays the bagpipes, small pipes, whistle and guitar. He started aged seven on the chanter (the part of the bagpipe resembling a recorder with

Seonaidh MacIntyre playing his bagpipes at Ceòlas
Ceòlas

finger holes to play the different notes) and he went on to become an accomplished bagpiper. Seonaidh sometimes pipes for Highland Dancers but more often accompanies Step Dancers, always ensuring that the grace notes or embellishments are secondary to the rhythm.

I noticed at the final Ceòlas ceilidh that Seonaidh and all the other pipers nodded respectfully to one person in the audience. This was an old lady with fine features sitting a few chairs along from me. During the interval I was introduced to her: Rona Lightfoot, born in 1936, a celebrated Scottish singer and bagpipe player. It is not just men who have the puff and

Rona Lightfoot, revered Scottish singer and bagpipe player. Unusually for bagpipers, Rona rests the pipes on her right shoulder
Photo courtesy of Archie Lightfoot

aptitude for the pipes. Dena Woodhams who organised the international reeling balls is another accomplished piper, as I heard when she played in Oman along with Mark Tennant and Alastair Campbell, all members of the London Pinstripe

Craigellachie Band, led by Ian Muir
Photo: Isobel McTear

Highlanders. For an earlier ball in Florence, Dena had mustered Pipe Majors Finlay MacDonald and Ian Duncan to set the scene for the ensuing reels.

The pipers then give way to Scottish dance bands – for example, Simon Howie's, Wayne Roberston's, Frank Reid's or the Pictish Players (the last being the regular troupe at the Northern Meeting). A popular band based in England is the Craigellachie, led by Ian Muir on the accordion with his wife, Judith, at the keyboard, plus two fiddles, drums and one more accordion. The six musicians play at ceilidhs, reels and Scottish Country Dances. Venues have included the Cheltenham Town Hall and Hurlingham Club (both with sprung wooden floors); a huge sports centre in the Shetland Islands; farmyard barns; and once, for a staff ceilidh, the basement of Buckingham Palace! It was just before Christmas and Ian recalls seeing the cakes Queen Elizabeth had ordered for her grandchildren, including a hedgehog one for little William. Another unusual place was a gymnasium in Kazan (for a Burns Night dance) which the mainly young Russian guests reached by travelling for three days by train.

Ian was also Music Director of the RSCDS (decades before Luke Brady) so is used to providing the strict tempo which most dancers favour. He has played outdoors for summertime RSCDS events at Polesden Lacey but finds it harder playing outside as there are no walls to make the music resound.

Whatever the venue, the Craigellachie are up for a challenge and enjoy travelling worldwide to accompany dancers, from youngsters to grandparents. Ian and Judith appreciate how inclusive Scottish dancing can be – and beautiful when danced impeccably. They also love the music itself: the melodies, the variety of pace and even the tricky pieces – 'General Stuart's Rant', for instance, or the better known 'Montgomeries' Rant' which, according to Ian, 'has lots of twiddly notes and is in B flat'.

CHAPTER TEN

The Gear: Kilts, Sporrans, Ghillies, Sgian Dubhs…

ALTHOUGH SCOTTISH DANCING can be done in shorts and trainers there is no doubt that tartan and the traditional paraphernalia make it more colourful and enjoyable. Unusually, the vibrant hues are for both sexes – unlike, say, Spanish Flamenco or Argentinian Tango where the men dress in black.

The main item for boys and men is, of course, the kilt. One outlet that has been making and selling kilts for decades – in fact, since 1868 – is Kinloch Anderson, the name of both the company (in Edinburgh) and the surname of its present director, John, the sixth generation of the family which established the business. John told me how they started as 'a gentleman's tailor' in George Street then expanded the kilt making during the First World War when the Black Watch and Highland regiments ordered thousands of kilts for the soldiers.

The demand for kilts has ebbed and flowed with flurries of orders for other garments – for instance, kilted skirts in the 1960s to 1980s. But there have always been people (including Highland Dancers) coming into the Kinloch Anderson store to buy their kilts. Orders from abroad came initially by letter, then telex, then fax and now emails. Video calls are useful so that the kilt-makers can see how customers are measuring

John Kinloch Anderson, 6th generation of the family business, Kinloch Anderson Ltd

Photo courtesy of Kinloch Anderson Ltd

themselves, maybe interjecting with an, 'Oh, that's not quite where we'd consider your waist to be.'

For those bewildered by the vast array of tartans the first question is, 'What's your name?' The surname might already have a tartan attached to it which would make that material the obvious choice for a kilt a customer is having made, enabling him to recognise distant cousins similarly attired at weddings or balls!

John Kinloch Anderson appreciates working in a sphere that is associated with cheerful occasions. He also takes pride in having devised the tartans and kilts for the British Caledonian crew as well as Glenlivet, Barbour, the University of St Andrews and Irn-Bru. But he acknowledges that much of the credit for his company's success is due to the skilful kilt-makers.

One of his star employees is Margaret Croy. She started as a seamstress at the age of 16, has been making kilts ever since and been working at Kinloch Anderson for over 20 years. She is one of the few making prized, hand-sewn kilts, deftly stitching all the pleats numbering, on average, 32 to 34 but rising to 40 pleats for a larger man. All kilts need an enormous length of material. When I met Margaret she had just finished a kilt for a small, five-year-old Highland Dancer. Even that required five yards of tartan. An average kilt has eight yards of material, a 40-pleat, larger one needs nine yards and for certain tartans with bigger 'setts' (pattern repeats) the kilt will have ten yards of fabric (9.1 metres).

Margaret and her associates can adjust garments to accommodate pot bellies or disguise limps or hollow backs.

Margaret Croy at work hand-stitching the pleats of a kilt
Photo courtesy of Kinloch Anderson Ltd

Such a 'bespoke' kilt, tailor-made for a specific individual, takes about three days to make whether the pleats are machine or hand stitched (and the latter costs more). The most expensive kilt, at around £1,325, would be a 'deluxe' or army one, taking a week to make because it has 'box' pleats (where you can put your hand in both sides of the pleat).

Whether a kilt is bespoke, made to measure or off the peg, it is likely to last several lifetimes. Margaret has tweaked kilts going back centuries and she pointed out that King Charles (for whom she has made various kilts) also wears kilts formerly worn by his grandfather. Prestigious though it is to sew for the royal family, Margaret's favourite customers are the 'wee girls' starting out in Highland Dancing. 'They come in all shy,' says Margaret, 'and are thrilled with the finished article.' A child's kilt has inbuilt spare material on either side of the 'apron' (the smooth front part of a kilt) so the garment can be let out as the child grows. The key thing for all kilts is that the lines of the tartan align in the pleats, and the pleats swish and swing whether they adorn a soldier on the march or a dancer in a spin.

Tradition has it that men wearing kilts do not wear underpants. I suspect most dancers prefer not to bare all when they swirl around so they dress accordingly. Modesty apart, men in kilts are expected to sport a sporran. They are otherwise deemed to be wearing skirts. Sporrans are useful anyway for putting keys, dance cards and crib sheets – items that men wearing Black or White Tie or tartan trews would carry in their pockets. (In the late 18th century, an elegant

Dancer sporting a lacy jabot
Photo courtesy of Dena Woodhams

Left: sporran (red fox) The Scotland Kilt Company
Right: the new dance fan for 1797 The Trustees of the British Museum

Lady in red at a glittering ball in Italy
Photo courtesy of Dena Woodhams

alternative to a scrappy crib sheet was a Dance Fan with the musical score and instructions for dances printed across the leaves of the fan.) Sporrans range from neat leather pouches to plump hairy beasts – made from mink, racoon, musquash, sealskin or assorted foxes. Other accessories include a kilt pin and Sgian Dubh (meaning 'black knife') which is normally worn down the right sock, though I observed one enterprising man using the same spot to tuck a much more useful fan! All reputable Highland Wear outlets sell or hire out the '11-piece package' comprising kilt, jacket, other garments (such as a 'jabot'), adornments and shoes.

Women, meanwhile, have always worn skirts or dresses, either slimline or full according to the fashion of the day, but usually long ones for balls. The fabrics currently in vogue

Display team from the Nottingham branch of the RSCDS wearing plain white dresses

Nottingham RSCDS

are unpatterned, bright coloured silks or tartan satins. In demonstration teams, however, women might wear plain white dresses. Over one shoulder, ladies often drape a plaid (tartan sash) which can be secured with a round brooch incorporating a stag or thistle or Celtic knot.

Highland Dancers, meanwhile, have their own distinctive attire. Their appearance really matters. A hair out of place, a sock that falls down, a crumpled kilt would lose them crucial points. Of paramount importance, too, is the Highland Dancer's shoes.

Tom and Linda Struthers run the St Andrews Shoemakers having bought the well-established James Senior shoe company in 2002. They continue to manufacture the same James Senior styles of shoe including ghillies for Highland Dancers. The ghillies' classic fingers of leather, through which the shoelaces run, enable the wearer to loosen or tighten every inch of the shoe so that it moulds onto the foot. But unlike regular ghillies, the ones the Struthers make for Highland Dancers have only a small bit of shock absorber at the front and none at the heel. This is because those younger dancers have a natural pad of fat on the ball of the foot so have less need of insoles which, they anyway maintain, would stop them having a feel for the ground.

Older Scottish Country Dancers have less fat underfoot, so the Struthers put thick shock absorbers into SCD shoes, whether ghillies or pumps. They are very much alive to the needs of customers. For instance, if somebody has a problematic Achilles tendon, they recommend half-inch heels. They noticed that New Zealanders, who often wear sandals or flip-flops, have broader feet than usual, so they manufacture wider-fitting dance shoes for them. For Highland Dancers who might incorporate the Irish Jig in their syllabus, they are making jig shoes with a hard leather sole which is fish scaled so that the shoe is both flexible and audible when tapped.

Pumps

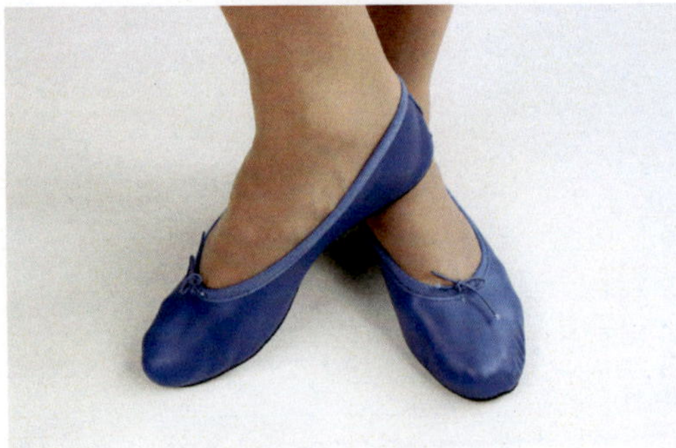

Ghillies

Jig shoes

All lined up
Photo: Isobel McTear

The traditional colour for dance shoes is black. But the St Andrews Shoemakers (and others) produce blue, red, green, burgundy or gold ones too. The leather must be supple and long-lasting. Tom Struthers explained that in hot countries the hides come from leaner cows so there is less fat in the leather, making it thinner and less durable. The best leather in the world comes from Italy, the UK and Argentina with the last being the first choice for Scottish dancing shoes.

So, Tom uses leather mainly from Argentina but also some tanned leather from Scotland depending on the sorts of shoe they are making. The shock absorber insoles come from England, the laces and eyelets from Germany and the shoes are cut and assembled in Agra, the epicentre of shoemaking in India and renowned for its fine quality of workmanship. Thus, a dancing shoe bought from St Andrews has a truly international provenance.

Proud though they are of their dancing shoes, Tom and Linda resort to trainers when they go to any ceilidhs. They have danced for decades, Linda being the great-niece of band leader Jimmy Shand, but are wary of boisterous dancers in hard or pointy shoes treading on their feet. For balls they would put on smarter shoes, but it is only at Scottish Country Dances where almost everyone is in soft shoes that they would wear their own ghillies or pumps.

So, there we have it. Go barefoot or clad in shoes that fit the dance and fellow dancers.

Then,

> 'Step we gaily on we go
> Heel for heel and toe for toe!'

Epilogue

THE LAST WORD should go to the essayist Thomas de Quincey, who recounts in his *Confessions of an English Opium-Eater* (1821) how much he relished the spectacle of Scottish dancing, describing its 'free, fluent and continuous motion' as 'a sort of masque of human life, with its whole equipage of pomps and glories, its luxury of sight and sound, its hours of golden youth, and the interminable revolution of ages hurrying after ages, and one generation treading over the flying footsteps of another.'

The next generation
Photo courtesy of Dena Woodhams

Shall We Dance?

Information on associations organising Scottish dancing, and useful booklets and websites.

SCOTTISH COUNTRY DANCING
Contact the Royal Scottish Country Dance Society (RSCDS), 12 Coates Crescent, Edinburgh EH3 7AF.
Tel: 0131 225 3854
Email: info@rscds.org
Website: www.rscds.org
The website has details of SCD classes and branches. There are 160 branches worldwide and over 200 affiliated groups. The RSCDS website also provides information on steps and techniques and has an online shop selling dance instruction booklets and accompanying music CDs.

REELING
London Reels meet once a month from September to June in the lower hall of St Columba's Church, Pont Street, London SW1X 0BD and once a year (usually in February) there is a ball at a top London venue, eg Grand Hall, Battersea Arts Centre.
Email: londonreels@gmail.com
Website: www.londonreels.co.uk

PGT (Parsons Green Tube) reels at Marlborough Primary School, Draycott Avenue, London SW3 3AP on Thursday evenings.
Website: www.pgtreels.com

There are several reeling groups across the UK including hampshirereels@gmail.com

Universities in Scotland (and elsewhere in UK) have reeling clubs.

Stockbridge Scottish Reelers meet on Monday evenings all year, except August, at 2 Cheyne Street, Edinburgh EH4 1JB.
Email: stockbridgereelers@gmail.com.

For reeling abroad, try Caledonian Societies and/or reeling websites for specific locations.

For reeling in New York, email: info@nyscottishball.com.

CEILIDHS

The London Ceilidh Club is a commercial organisation hosting three-hour ceilidhs for about £20 per person at Cecil Sharp House, 2 Regent's Park Road, London NW1 7AY and other venues.
Website: www.ceilidhclub.org.

Licence to Ceilidh (based in London) organises bands and callers for weddings and parties.
Tel: 07855-050-778
Email: info@licencetoceilidh.com

HotScotch Ceilidh Band organise ceilidhs, including for weddings, anywhere in Scotland.
Website: www.myceilidh.co.uk

'Ceilidh Callers for hire near you' represents Frank Reid, John Carver, Ian Robertson and many others providing caller and/or band.
Website: www.encoremusicians.com

GAY GORDONS

Mainly SCD but also reeling and ceilidh dancing for the LGBTQI+ community in –
Manchester: www.gay-gordons-manchester.co.uk
Edinburgh: www.evocredbook.org.uk
Email: info@gaygordonsedinburgh.com
London: www.thegaygordons.org or via RSCDS website.
Classes every Wednesday in Islington and sometimes at St Columba's, Pont Street SW1X 0BD.

HIGHLAND DANCING

The Royal Scottish Official Board of Highland Dancing (RSOBHD) is the world governing body of Highland Dancing.
Headquarters: 32 Grange Loan, Edinburgh EH9 2NR.
Tel: 0131-668-3965
Email: admin@rsobhd.net
Website: www.rsobhd.net

The Scottish Official Highland Dancing Association (SOHDA) has lists of dance schools in several Scottish cities.
Website: www.sohda.co.uk

New Zealand Academy of Highland and National Dancing Inc, PO Box 5470, Palmerston, New Zealand.
Website: www.nzahnd.org

Piping & Dancing Association of New Zealand
Email: pipinganddancing@xtra.co.nz
Website: www.piping-dancing.org.nz

The Official Board of Highland Dancing South Africa (OBHDSA)
Website: www.highlanddancing.co.za

STEP DANCE

Mabou School of Cape Breton Step Dance, Nova Scotia – runs a week-long course in July and has online Step Dance instruction videos.
Tel: 00-1-902-595-0794
www.capebretonstepdance.com

Ceòlas, Cnoc Soilleir, Dalabrog, South Uist, HS8 5SS – runs a week-long course in July for intermediate and advanced Step Dancers.
Tel: 01878-790600
Email: info@Ceòlas.co.uk
www.ceolas.co.uk

Sabhal Mòr Ostaig, Sleat, Isle of Skye, Scotland, IV44 8RQ – runs occasional Step Dance courses.
Tel: 01471 888 000 (general enquiries)
Email: fios@smo.uhi.ac.uk
Website: www.smo.uhi.ac.uk

Admissions/course information:
Tel: 01471 888 304
Email: iarrtas@smo.uhi.ac.uk

Kelvingrove Dancers with teacher, Kae Sakurai – weekly Step Dance classes on Thursday evenings at SDTA Studios, 1st Floor, 101 Park Road, Glasgow, G4 9JE. Also online instruction via Zoom
Website: www.kelvingrovedancers.com.

Sophie Stephenson – see www.sophabulous.co.uk for schedule of live performances and workshops plus online Step Dance classes. Sophie also offers one-to-one and small group lessons at Sgoil Dannsa Scottish Step Dance studio in Inverness.

USEFUL BOOKS AND CDS

The Swinging Sporran by Roddy Martine and Andrew Campbell (Birlinn Ltd).

Collins Pocket Reference *Scottish Country Dancing* by Peter Knight, compiled in association with RSCDS (Harper Collins).

RSCDS dance booklets and CDs via www.rscds.org
eg Book 48 contains detailed instructions and diagrams for 15 Scottish Country Dances with full piano scores for the original tunes. Book 48 CD has music, arranged by George Meikle, to accompany the 15 dances.

A Guide to SCD vol 1 has popular ceilidh dances ('Gay Gordons', 'Lambeth Walk', 'Britannia Two Step'…)

A Guide to SCD vol 2 has all the main reels and 'Posties Jig', 'Strip the Willow', 'Waltz Country Dance', 'Petronella'…

ONLINE

www.scottish-country-dancing-dictionary.com has instructions for hundreds of dances, plus crib sheets and links to YouTube videos of many dances with instructions voiced by Alastair Pettigrew.

www.londonreels.co.uk has video tutorials of the reels practised regularly at Pont Street, London, created by John Carver (former chairman of London Reels).

NOTE

The people running committees and organisations often change hands. Likewise, there are changes in the schedules and venues of dance lessons, courses and events. Please check with relevant associations for up-to-date information.

Bibliography

Scottish Dance Beyond 1805 by Patricia Ballantyne (Routledge, 2019).

A Social History of Scottish Dance by George Emmerson (McGill-Queen's University Press, 1972).

Scottish Country Dancing edited by Peter Knight, compiled in association with RSCDS (Harper Collins, 1996).

Highland Balls and Village Halls by GW Lockhart (Luath Press, 1985).

Dance With Your Soul by Alastair MacFadyen (Royal Scottish Country Dance Society, 1983).

101 Scottish Country Dances compiled by Jean Milligan (Collins, 1956).

The Swinging Sporran by Roddy Martine and Andrew Campbell (Wolfe Publishing 1973, later Birlinn).

Scots in India by Dena Woodhams (Yinbound Books & Blurb, 2014).

Scots in Italy by Dena Woodhams (Yinbound Books/Federighi, 2016).

Scots in Oman by Dena Woodhams (Yinbound Books & Blurb, 2018).

'Toast to the Laddies'

HERE IS SOME doggerel I wrote to wind up my 'Toast to the Laddies' at one Burns Night:

What is the appeal
Of laddies who reel?
Is it, in part, what they wear?
I mean the whole gear,
Right up to the hilt,
With sporran and kilt
And tucked in the hose a 'sgian dubh'
(Or 'black knife' to me and to you);
And others who choose
To wear tartan trews –
In trousers or kilts they look fine;
And if they pay for the wine
It serves to remind
Us lasses how kind
The male of the species can be
And not in the leastie
The sort of beastie
Who's cowering, timorous or wee.
No, the laddies stand tall,
The beaux of the ball;
It's stags they resemble, not mice!
And they're vigorous, jolly and nice.
So here is my answer:
A male who's a dancer
And reels is a thing of great joy
Whether he be a man or a boy.

Without further ado
I call upon you
Who are lasses to stand up and cheer
The gorgeous, fit lads who are here!

Author's Note

SINCE I STARTED writing this book, a few individuals I have profiled or mentioned have sadly died. Amongst them are Edith Campbell of Wellington, New Zealand, who passed away of 24 September 2024, and Daniel Capron who died on 19 May 2025. But the spirit of the deceased lives on in the minds of their fellow dancers and in the pages of this book.

Acknowledgements

THE MAIN PEOPLE I would like to thank are those whom I interviewed for this book. There are scores of them and they all gave up their time to patiently answer my questions. Many of them supplied images too. Dena Woodhams generously allowed me to use dozens of the photographs she had commissioned for the balls she organised worldwide. Roddy Martine gave me the go-ahead to use a couple of his *Swinging Sporran* cartoons, as well as drawing sketches of Jean Milligan especially for my book.

But there were also people behind the scenes who were helpful in giving me information about the specific genres of dance. Shiobhan Smith, in Otago, New Zealand, explained the differences between Highland Dancing in her own country and elsewhere – as well as relaying her photos of Highland dancers and the contact details of other dance photographers. Rod Downey, also from New Zealand, filled me in on Scottish Country Dancing in his country. Pat Ballantyne in Delft, the Netherlands, and Margie Beaton in Cape Breton, Nova Scotia, described the history and distinctive features of Step Dance. The St Andrew's Society of Toronto outlined the reeling at their annual ball and dispatched photos of it. Emilie Greener, the secretary of the Royal Caledonian Ball, relayed how that charity ball originated. Peter Knight lent me all his books on the history of Scottish dancing.

I could not have assembled all the photographs without the unstinting help of Lyndsay Walker and Alan Macpherson at the RSCDS, Elizabeth Golan of the RSOBHD and Peggy Ann Macmillan at Ceòlas where I went to learn Step Dance. Alissia Gocan-Wright relayed some charming photos of her children at Cowal as well as their views on Highland Dancing. Past and present members of the London Reels and Perth Ball committees sourced excellent photos from their files, as did the Hurlingham Club in London. Honing images, cropping some, arranging all of them in the right order were huge tasks. I have my sister, Virginia Knowles, to thank for downloading photos and I am indebted to Cosima Gibbs, Nicki Stenning and Trevor Ager for fine-tuning all the images on my computer.

Sue Porter, running the RSCDS Summer School which I attended, introduced me to fellow students from near and far and found rooms where I could interview them.

An old associate and literary agent, Caroline Dawnay, took the trouble to read the draft of *Heel for Heel* and came up with some constructive suggestions. Rosie Friis improved the structure of the text for which I am very grateful. I am also indebted to all the team at Luath.

Finally, I would like to thank my daughter, Jessica, who read the first version of the book and said she enjoyed it. She encouraged me to keep going to the very end – which I have because this is it!

Luath Press Limited

committed to publishing well written books worth reading

LUATH PRESS takes its name from Robert Burns, whose little collie Luath (*Gael.*, swift or nimble) tripped up Jean Armour at a wedding and gave him the chance to speak to the woman who was to be his wife and the abiding love of his life. Burns called one of the 'Twa Dogs' Luath after Cuchullin's hunting dog in Ossian's *Fingal*. Luath Press was established in 1981 in the heart of Burns country, and is now based a few steps up the road from Burns' first lodgings on Edinburgh's Royal Mile. Luath offers you distinctive writing with a hint of unexpected pleasures.

ILLUSTRATION: IAN KELLAS

Most bookshops in the UK, the US, Canada, Australia, New Zealand and parts of Europe, either carry our books in stock or can order them for you. To order direct from us, please send a £sterling cheque, postal order, international money order or your credit card details (number, address of cardholder and expiry date) to us at the address below. Please add post and packing as follows: UK – £1.00 per delivery address; overseas surface mail – £2.50 per delivery address; overseas airmail – £3.50 for the first book to each delivery address, plus £1.00 for each additional book by airmail to the same address. If your order is a gift, we will happily enclose your card or message at no extra charge.

Luath Press Limited
543/2 Castlehill
The Royal Mile
Edinburgh EH1 2ND
Scotland
Telephone: 0131 225 4326 (24 hours)
Email: sales@luath.co.uk
Website: www.luath.co.uk